THE PEOPLE NAMED
THE CHIPPEWA

∎

Anishinaabe woman, about
1890. Photo courtesy of
Minnesota Historical Society.

THE PEOPLE NAMED THE CHIPPEWA

NARRATIVE HISTORIES

∎

Gerald Vizenor

UNIVERSITY OF MINNESOTA PRESS □ MINNEAPOLIS

Published by the University of Minnesota
Press, 2037 University Avenue Southeast,
Minneapolis, MN 55414
Printed in the United States of America.

The author expresses his gratitude to the
Graduate School of the University of
Minnesota for research funds to complete
this book.

*Library of Congress Cataloging in Publication
Data*

Vizenor, Gerald Robert, 1934-
  The people named the Chippewa.

  Bibliography: p.
  Includes index.
  1. Chippewa Indians—History. 2. Chip-
pewa Indians—Biography. I. Title.
E99.C6V593   1984   970.004'97   83-19800
ISBN 0-8166-1305-2
ISBN 0-8166-1306-0 (pbk.)

The University of Minnesota
is an equal opportunity
educator and employer.

9522812

In Memory of
Alice Beaulieu Vizenor

■

The Ojibways affirm that long before they became aware of the white man's presence on this continent, their coming was prophesied by one of their old men, whose great sanctity and oft-repeated fasts enabled him to commune with spirits and see far into the future. He prophesied that the white spirits would come in numbers like sand on the lake shore, and would sweep the red race from the hunting grounds which the Great Spirit had given them as an inheritance. It was prophesied that the consequences of the white man's appearance would be, to the Anishinaabeg, *an ending of the world.*

William Whipple Warren
History of the Ojibway Nation

CONTENTS

Anishinaabeg (Chippewa) Reservations in Minnesota and Wisconsin

Reservations

1. White Earth
2. Leech Lake
3. Mille Lacs
4. Nett Lake
5. Fond du Lac
6. Grand Portage

7. Red Lake
8. Bad River
9. Red Cliff
10. Lac du Flambeau
11. Lac Courte Oreille
12. Skokaogon - Mole Lake

THE PEOPLE NAMED
THE CHIPPEWA

■

PROLOGUE

■

We are what we imagine. Our very existence consists in our imagination of ourselves. . . . The greatest tragedy that can befall us is to go unimagined.
N. Scott Momaday,
Indian Voices

■

Odinigun, an elder from the White Earth Reservation, told about the woodland trickster and the creation of the first earth. The people on the first earth were not wise, "they had no clothing . . . they sat around and did nothing. Then the spirit of the creator sent a man to teach them. . . . The first thing he taught them was how to make a fire by means of a bow and stick and a bit of decayed wood. . . . Then he taught them how to cook meat by the fire. They had no axes, but he took a pole and burned it in two over the fire. He taught them to boil meat in fresh birch bark. It was a long time before they had things as he wanted them, but after a while they were made comfortable by his help. They had no minds or ideas of their own. . . ."

This was the time before the appearance of Naanabozho, the woodland trickster, on the first earth. The spirit teacher told the first people on the earth that they "must fast and find out things by dreams and that if they paid attention to these dreams they would learn how to heal the sick. The people listened and fasted and found in dreams how to teach their children and do everything. The young men were taught that they must regulate their lives by dreams, they must live normal lives, be industrious, and be moderate in the use of tobacco when it should be given to them. They were especially taught that their minds would not be clear if they ate and drank too much. . . ." The spirit teacher taught them how to use tobacco and corn.

Naanabozho, the compassionate woodland trickster, wanders in mythic time and transformational space between tribal experiences and dreams. The trickster is related to plants and animals and trees; he is a

3

teacher and healer in various personalities who, as numerous stories reveal, explains the values of healing plants, wild rice, maple sugar, basswood, and birch bark to woodland tribal people. More than a magnanimous teacher and transformer, the trickster is capable of violence, deceptions, and cruelties: the realities of human imperfections. The woodland trickster is an existential shaman in the comic mode, not an isolated and sentimental tragic hero in conflict with nature.

The trickster is comic in the sense that he does not reclaim idealistic ethics, but survives as a part of the natural world; he represents a spiritual balance in a comic drama rather than the romantic elimination of human contradictions and evil.

Naanabozho lived in the woodland with Nookomis, which, in the oral tradition, means *grandmother*. The various mythic genealogies on the trickster reveal that he had a twin brother and that his mother either died or disappeared when the peripatetic comic figure was born. When the trickster learned from his grandmother that his mother was taken from the woodland by a powerful wind spirit, he set out to find her somewhere in a strange and distant place on the earth.

Nookomis warned her trickster grandson that the distant land he intended to visit was infested with hideous humans and "evil spirits and the followers of those who eat human flesh."

"No one who has ever been within their power has ever been known to return," she told her grandson. "First these evil spirits charm their victims by the sweetness of their songs, then they strangle and devour them, but your principle enemy will be the great gambler who has never been beaten in his game and who lives beyond the realm of darkness. . . . Therefore, my grandson, I would beseech you not to undertake so dangerous a journey."

Naanabozho listened to his grandmother, but the woodland trickster knew no fear in the world. The warning words of his grandmother were unheeded.

Naanabozho first traveled in a birch bark canoe, the first one ever made on the earth, and as he searched for his mother he encountered different animals and birds and spirits. He consulted with the birds and animals and good spirits and it was decided that the owl would lend the trickster his eyes and the firefly would travel with him to light the way through the realms of darkness, where he would encounter the evil gambler. He paddled to the end of the woodland; then he took a path that led him through swamps and over high mountains and by deep chasms in the earth where he saw the hideous stare of a thousand gleaming eyes . . . and he heard the groans and hisses and yells of countless fiends gloating over their many victims of sin and shame . . . and he knew that this was the place where the great gambler had abandoned the spirits of his victims who had lost the game.

Naanabozho approached the entrance of the wigwam and raised the mat of scalps that served as the door. Inside he found himself in the presence of the great gambler, who was a curious being, a person who seemed almost round in shape, smooth and white.

"So, Naanabozho, you too have come to try your luck, and you think I am not a very expert gambler," the great gambler said, reaching for his war club and chuckling a horrible sound of scorn and ridicule. His round white shape shivered.

"All of these hands you see hanging around this wigwam are the hands of your people who came here to gamble. They thought as you are now thinking, they played and lost their lives.

"I seek no one to come and gamble with me but those who would gamble their lives. Remember that I demand the lives of those who gamble with me and lose. I keep the scalps and ears and hands, and the rest of the bodies are given to my friends the flesh eaters. . . . The spirit of those who have lost their lives I consign to the land of darkness," the great gambler said, still grinning with confidence. His flesh seemed moist, like a poison mushroom. "Now I have spoken and we will play the game of the four ages of man."

The great gambler took in his stout hands the dish game and said this to the woodland trickster: "Here are the four figures, the four ages of man, which I will shake in the dish four times, and if they assume a standing position each time, then I am the winner. . . . Should they fall, then you are the winner."

"Very well, we will play," Naanabozho said, his words wedged in nervous laughter. "But it is customary for the party who is challenged to play any game to have the last play." The trickster looked down at the dish and the figures of the four ages of man. The great gambler shivered in the realm of darkness.

The gambler consented to the invitation of the trickster as he took the dish and struck it to the ground for the first time. The four figures remained in the standing position. This was repeated twice more by the great gambler and each time the four figures representing the four ages of man remained in the standing position in the dish. The power of evil was not threatened.

The destinies of the trickster and tribal people of the woodland depended upon the one chance remaining, the last throw of the dish. Should the figures of the four ages of man come down in the standing position then the trickster would lose and the spirit of tribal people would be consigned to the *wiindigoo*, the flesh eaters in the land of darkness.

When the gambler prepared to make the final shake of the game, the woodland trickster drew near and when the dish came down to the ground he made a teasing whistle on the wind and all four figures of the ages of man fell in the darkness of the dish. The great gambler shivered, his flesh seemed to harden and break into small pieces when he looked up toward the trickster.

Naanabozho smiled at the great gambler. The woodland tribes had not lost their spirit to the land of darkness. The trickster had stopped evil for a moment in a game. "Now it is my turn," the woodland trickster said to the great gambler, "and should I win, should all the four ages of man stand in the dish, then you will lose your life. . . ."

Naanabozho cracked the dish on the earth.

TRADITIONAL ORIGINS

∎

Civilization is an affair of story telling. . . . Because the adventurer is fully alive only when he acts, he is a man without a past. Each episode is for him a fresh identity, a beginning of sorts. . . . By recalling, and telling, his adventures, he defeats time, inserting his past lives into the present.

Paul Zweig,
The Adventurer

∎

The woodland creation stories are told from visual memories and ecstatic strategies, not from scriptures. In the oral tradition, the mythic origins of tribal people are creative expressions, original eruptions in time, not a mere recitation or a recorded narrative in grammatical time. The teller of stories is an artist, a person of wit and imagination, who relumes the diverse memories of the visual past into the experiences and metaphors of the present. The past is familiar enough in the circles of the seasons, woodland places, lake and rivers, to focus a listener on an environmental metaphor and an intersection where the earth started in mythic time, where a trickster or a little woodland person stopped to imagine the earth. The tribal creation takes place at the time of the telling in the oral tradition; the variations in mythic stories are the imaginative desires of tribal artists.

Karl Kroeber, editor of *Traditional Literatures of the American Indian*, writes that "anthropologists and folklorists, whose disciplines are not directed toward appreciation of superior artistry, usually play down, or ignore, the individual distinction of creative accomplishment in ethnographic material." In the same book, Dennis Tedlock explains that the "teller is not merely repeating memorized words, nor is he or she merely giving a dramatic 'oral interpretation' or 'concert reading' of a fixed script.

We are in the presence of a *performing art*, all right, but we are getting the *criticism* at the same time and from the same person. The interpreter does not merely play the parts, but is the narrator and commentator as well."

Walter Ong, in *Orality and Literacy*, writes about the differences between oral cultures and written words, the changes in thought processes and the transformation of consciousness. "Oral speech is fully natural to human beings in the sense that every human being in every culture . . . learns to talk.

"Writing or script differs as such from speech in that it does not inevitably well up out of the unconscious. The process of putting spoken language into writing is governed by consciously contrived, articulable rules. . . . Thought is nested in speech, not in texts, all of which have their meanings through reference of the visible symbol to the world of sound. . . . The spoken word is always an event, a movement in time, completely lacking in the thing-like repose of the written or printed word. . . . Writing and print isolate.

"Thinking of oral tradition or a heritage of oral performance, genres and styles as 'oral literature' is rather like thinking of horses as automobiles without wheels," Ong writes. "This is to say, a literate person cannot fully recover a sense of what the word is to purely oral people."

Odinigun, for example, told Frances Densmore, who published his stories in *Chippewa Customs*, that the woodland trickster was born after the first people on earth had learned how to dream and to make fire, which is not the same as other stories about the trickster as earthdiver. The variations are the work of imagination, not disagreement. Odinigun is an artist, not a scrivener; he does not recount a standardized historical narrative for the pleasure of culture cultists and methodologists.

Victor Barnouw, an anthropologist, collected earthdiver creation stories at Lac du Flambeau and published them in *Wisconsin Chippewa Myths and Tales*. The narrator of the following trickster myth is a shaman, Barnouw writes, a tribal spiritual leader, "to whom I have given the pseudonym of Tom Badger . . . a quite level-headed man in his seventies, with a good sense of humor." Badger, an artist, tells the following about the trickster:

"The story that I'm going to tell you won't be about this earth. It will be about a different world. There were only two people living in this other world: an old lady and her daughter. Look how this world looks around us—trees, flowers, and everything. In this other world there was only grass and bushes, no timber.

"The old lady's daughter used to go every day into the woods to find something that she could use for food. This was in the summer. She got those early berries that come in the spring. That was their food. She went into the woods to pick the ripe berries all day long, picking here and there. Then one day somebody saw her traveling all alone by herself in the woods. That person seemed to take a liking to her. He even wanted to marry her. He knew what to do. When she was out berrying one nice hot day, when there was no wind, at noon-time, she heard a noise like a gust of wind. She looked around in the direction of the noise and saw a wind coming. When the wind reached her, she couldn't pull her dress down for some time, until the gust of wind went by. She didn't think anything of it, because no one was there to see her. She started picking berries again. . . . It wasn't long afterwards that the girl found out that something else was going to happen. She left that place where she and her mother had been living and went into the woods. There she gave birth to some children — three of them. The first looked just like a human baby boy. After it was born, she held him in her arms. . . . Then the next baby was born. This one didn't have human features exactly, but he looked like a human baby to some extent. Just a little while later another one was born. This one didn't look like a human child. This one was a stone. . . .

"The trickster was the first-born child.

"Naanabozho was standing on the top of the tree . . . and the water was up to his mouth. Pretty soon Naanabozho felt that he wanted to defecate. He couldn't hold it. The shit floated up to the top of the water and floated around his mouth. . . .

"Naanabozho noticed that there was an animal in the water. . . . Then he saw several animals — beaver, muskrat, and otter. Naanabozho spoke to the otter first.

" 'Brother,' he said, 'could you go down and get some earth? If you do that, I will make an earth for you and me to live on. . . .' The otter did not find the earth.

"Naanabozho asked the other animals to dive beneath the water. The muskrat returned with some earth in his paws. Then the trickster took the grains of sand in the palm of his hand and held them up to the sun to dry them out. When the sand was all dry, he threw it around onto the water. There was a little island then."

Naanabozho also appeared in stories published in *The Progress*, a newspaper edited by Theodore H. Beaulieu and published on the White Earth Reservation before the turn of the last century. These stories about the compassionate trickster were written by the mixedblood editor of the tribal newspaper; other stories about traditional culture and spiritual societies were attributed to tribal elders who told them in the oral tradition. The following events, however, were not translated but were written by the editor for publication in *The Progress*:

A great many winters since this country was occupied and owned exclusively by the Anishinaabeg woodland tribal people and other tribal peoples, there lived on the shores of a large lake, with his band, a powerful but unprincipled chief, who had a son who besides being as unprincipled as his father, was a profligate and despised by his people.

In the same *oodena*, or village, there lived a widow with a daughter who was a virgin pure and beautiful, with whom the chief's son was infatuated, but whose advances were repulsed by the maiden. Finally, tiring of the repeated failures of his suit, he decided to rely on his prerogative as the son of a chief, by having a wife selected by his father whose requests or commands would have to be obeyed by the parents or guardians of any Anishinaabeg in the band in the selection of a wife for the son. He informed his father of his desire to secure as his wife the girl in question. In due time, the chief sent the customary presents to her mother with a demand for her daughter as a wife for his son, but the widow refused this, and with her daughter made her escape from the *oodena*.

After traveling five days and five nights without camping, they arrived at a beautiful lake where the widow decided to build a wigwam and live permanently. For some unaccountable reason, the *manidoo*, the spirit, ignored and excluded the presence of man from this vicinity, which seemed to have been the meeting grounds of the four powerful *manidoog*, the spirits, representing the four winds.

One day while the young girl was gathering *manoomin*, wild rice, the *giiwedin manidoo*, the north spirit, who chanced to be passing by, spied her and became very much enamored of her. When she returned home, she related to her mother what she had observed. The latter became very much alarmed and warned her daughter to be very neat about her dress and person, and to guard against the wiles of the *giiwedin manidoo*, who was a very harsh fellow and might carry her off. Some days after this the young girl went into the woods to gather blueberries that grew in abundance along the banks of a brook that ran through a beautiful grove of pine trees.

While she was busily engaged gathering berries, the *giiwedin manidoo* in a very noisy and boisterous manner came to her, took her in his arms and kissed her, fluttered her garments, and then departed from whence he had come. For some time, the young girl was overcome with a delicious feeling of joy and happiness and she reclined to rest.

When she awoke from this delicious stupor, every tree in the forest was mingling its voice with the birds in piping forth their sweetest songs. When she returned home, she related to her mother what had taken place.

Her mother listened to this in silence and when the young girl concluded, said: *my daughter, this was foreordained.*

The young girl knew she had conceived and would become a mother.
In the course of time she became very sick and for several days she lay
in pain on a couch of boughs.

One day, feeling a little better than usual, she went outside and lay
down beneath the shade of a balsam tree. While resting thus, she heard
voices talking as if they were in dispute, and at the same time the sweet
tones of a nightingale were heard, as if endeavoring to pacify the
disputants. Suddenly there was a rustle, and a great gust of wind from
the north swept by and taking the young girl in his embrace disappeared
from the earth. The girl's mother, who had been enjoying a nap, was
awakened by the commotion, looked about the wigwam for her daughter,
and, being satisfied she was not within, hurried outside searching and
calling for her beloved child, but the sweet tones of the nightingale were
the only sounds that answered her call. At last, worn and with grief and
weeping, she returned to her now lonely wigwam, and while passing
the tree under which her daughter had so lately reclined, she overheard
a wee little voice say: *Nookomis, grandmother, do not cry. I am your grandchild and have been left here to comfort and to take care of you. My name is
Naanabozho and I shall be many things for the comfort of you and my people,
and when my work is done, I will take you home to your daughter, my mother,
where you will never be parted from her again.*

Sister Bernard Coleman, Ellen Frogner, and Estelle Eich, in *Ojibwa
Myths and Legends*, write that the stories "reflect the interests and con-
cerns that can be found in folk literature throughout the world and thus
they attain a universality. All this we found at our very door, but the time
for such finding is at an edge, and therefore a mid-twentieth century
record has special significance." The following translated version of the
birth of the trickster is attributed to an old tribal woman.

"Naanabozho had no mother. He lived with his grandmother. This
is how it was. . . . One day Naanabozho's mother went out with her
mother to get wood. After a while, the mother missed her daughter. There
was a very high wind. She looked for her daughter, but she could not
find her.

Later when the grandmother was chopping wood, she found a little
blood on one of the pieces. She brought the piece of wood into the
wigwam. She knew the blood was her daughter's. The next morning there
was a little baby. That was the beginning of Naanabozho's life, and he
lived with his grandmother.

Naanabozho was very curious about his parents. So he asked his grandmother. "The four corners of the wind killed your mother," she said. Then Naanabozho was angry. He wanted to find his mother, but his grandmother said, "No, she was blown to pieces." Naanabozho built a canoe of birch bark. "I'm going to find out who killed my mother and why."

He took his canoe out on Lake Superior and he called up a wind. He had power to talk to everything, animals, trees, wind, and everything. He remembered that his grandmother had warned him, "There is a powerful man out there that you will never be able to reach. There is a heavy gum on the water and you will never be able to get through it."

But as it turned out, Naanabozho had the power to go through it, and he finally reached the powerful man. This man knew that Naanabozho was coming for him.

This is true, this is the beginning of the story of Naanabozho and I am telling you. . . .

THE PEOPLE NAMED THE CHIPPEWA

∎

The Red Man died hating the white man. What remnant of him lives, lives hating the white man. . . . A curious thing about the Spirit of Place is the fact that no place exerts its full influence upon a new-comer until the old inhabitant is dead or absorbed.
D. H. Lawrence,
Studies in
Classic American Literature

∎

LANGUAGE AND NAMES

∎

In the language of the tribal past, the families of the woodland spoke of themselves as the Anishinaabeg until the colonists named them the Ojibway and Chippewa. The word Anishinaabeg, the singular is Anishinaabe, is a phonetic transcription from the oral tradition. Tribal people used the word Anishinaabeg to refer to the people of the woodland who spoke the same language. The collective name was not an abstract concept of personal identities or national ideologies. Tribal families were the basic political and economic units in the woodland and the first source of personal identities.

Individuals were given special names, dream names, at birth. These names were sacred and were not revealed to strangers. An individual was known in the traditional tribal world by a personal nickname; several names were given in some families, and with each nickname there were stories to be told. In the traditional past, a person in the tribe was selected to present a sacred name to a child. The parents gave nicknames, but a sacred name, a dream name, was a ceremonious event.

Frances Densmore, in *Chippewa Customs*, writes that "soon after the birth of a child its parents selected a person to name the child. This person was called a namer and usually gave to the child a name connected

13

with his or her dream. The bestowing of a name was not, however, the principal function of a namer. Indeed, the giving of a name was sometimes omitted. The principal function was the transmission to the child of the benefit which he or she derived from his or her dream.

"Odinigun, who had named several children, said that he always took the child in his arms and pressed it close to his body. He said that every namer did not do this, but he believed that more power was transmitted to the child by this action. A child was given power by its namer, but it rested somewhat with the child whether this power was developed. . . ."

Dream names were received from a name giver, or from a dream event. "The dream name acquired by an individual was usually received in the fast and isolation attendant upon the period of puberty and was associated with the tutelary spirit he acquired at that time. . . . This name was seldom mentioned.

"The experience of this dream gave its possessor a spirit power or protection which he could transmit to others, bestowing at the same time either his own dream name or some name which he composed from the incidents of his dream."

The nicknames, Densmore points out, were "short and frequently contained an element of humor. A child might be given a name derived from some circumstance at the time of its birth, or it might be named from the first person or animal that entered the lodge after its birth. Children were sometimes named from a fancied resemblance to something." Julia Spears, for example, was given the nickname Conians, which means "little money" in translation, "because her face was so round when she was born that it reminded the people of a small piece of silver money." Nicknames and descriptive names, but not dream names received in ceremonies, were transcribed and translated by missionaries and government officials as tribal surnames. In federal schools, however, tribal children were given arbitrary first and last names.

The Anishinaabeg are known to most of the world as the Ojibway and Chippewa; lexicon entries seldom explain the meaning of the different names. *The American Heritage Dictionary of the English Language,* for example, defines Ojibwa as a "tribe of Algonquin speaking North American Indians inhabiting regions of the United States and Canada around Lake Superior. . . . Also called 'Chippewa,' and 'Chippeway.' "

John Nichols, an editor with Earl Nyholm of *Ojibwewi-Ikidowinan: An Ojibwe Word Resource Book,* writes that the "Ojibwe language is one language of a wide-spread family of North American Indian languages known as the Algonquian language family, one of many such families of languages. Ojibwe is spoken by perhaps forty-thousand to fifty-

Anishinaabe man, about
1900. Photo courtesy of
Minnesota Historical Society.

thousand people in the north-central part of the continent. Although the English name 'Chippewa' is commonly used both for the people and their ancestral language in Michigan, Minnesota, North Dakota, and Wisconsin, in the language itself the people are the *Anishinaabeg* and the language is called *Anishinaabemowin* or *Ojibwemowin*. . . ."

Frances Densmore points out that the name "Chippewa is comparatively modern and is the only name under which the tribe has been designated by the government in treaties and other negotiations, but it has never been adopted by the older members of the tribe. They still refer to themselves as 'Ojibway,' or use the still older terms," Anishinaabe and the plural form Anishinaabeg.

'Chippewa' is still used in written references to the tribe. The Minnesota Chippewa Tribe, and the Minnesota Chippewa Tribal Council, for example, are the official corporate names for the representative tribal government on six reservations in the state. In the past decade, however, numerous new tribal organizations, most of them in urban areas, have made use of tribal words transcribed from the oral tradition. "Migizi Communications," for example, a tribal news service, means "bald eagle" in translation. The "Anishinabe Dee-Bah-Gee-Mo-Win," a section of the tribal newspaper from the White Earth Reservation, is a phonetic transcription of the two words in the oral tradition that mean, in translation: stories, or a narration of events of the people. Nichols and Nyholm transcribe these words as *Anishinaabe Dibaajimowin*. These variations in transcription are common, showing the differences in regional pronunciation of tribal words as well as the distance between the oral tradition and written languages. The oral tradition has no lexicon, of course; speakers remember what is heard and repeated. Written languages must impose what appears to be standard pronunciation when, in fact, most spoken sounds are seldom in absolute agreement with written words.

John Nichols writes that "Ojibwe and the other languages grouped together in the Algonquian language family resemble each other so closely in sound patterns, grammar, and vocabulary that at one time they must have been a single language: as the speakers of this ancient language, no longer spoken, became separated from one another, the way they spoke changed in different ways until we have the distinct languages spoken today. . . . At the time of the European invasion of North America, the languages of the Algonquian language family were spoken by Indians along the Atlantic coast from what is now North Carolina to Newfoundland, inland across Canada to the Great Plains, and in the region of the Great Lakes, perhaps ranging as far south as Alabama and Georgia. . . . Long contact with English and French, numerically more numerous and officially dominant, has taken its toll of many of these

The Big Bear family and
friends, about 1915. Photo
courtesy of Saint Paul
Dispatch.

languages. The condition of Ojibwe varies widely. In much of Northwestern and Northern Ontario and in Manitoba it is spoken by people
of all ages and the actual number of speakers is increasing as the population grows. In many Ojibwe communities in the United States and other
parts of Canada it is spoken only by those middle-aged and older. . . ."

More than a century ago, Henry Rowe Schoolcraft, a student of
geology and mineralogy and ethnology, named the Anishinaabeg the
Ojibwa; he reasoned that the root meaning of the word Ojibway described
the peculiar sound of the Anishinaabe voice. Schoolcraft served the Lewis
Cass expedition to Lake Superior as a geologist; later he claimed that he
discovered the source of the Mississippi at Lake Itasca, an arrogant assertion since he asked tribal people to direct him to the source of the river.
Schoolcraft married a tribal woman and wrote several books about tribal
culture. Henry Wadsworth Longfellow, the poet and romancer, was impressed with his work and copied his errors: Longfellow confused the
trickster Naanabozho with the Iroquois Hiawatha and placed his romantic narrative on the shores of Lake Superior.

George Copway, also known as Kahgegagahbowh, one of the first Anishinaabe Christian missionaries, explained that the woodland tribes were called the Ojibway because of the moccasins they wore, which were "gathered on the top from the tip of the toe, and at the ankle."

In *The Traditional History and Characteristic Sketches of the Ojibway Nation*, published in London in 1850, Kahgegagahbowh wrote that "no other Indians wore this style of foot-gear, and it was on account of this peculiarity that they were called Ojibway, the signification of which is *gathering*."

William Warren takes exception to both definitions of the word *Ojibway*. In his *History of the Ojibway Nation*, Warren, who was the first person of Anishinaabe heritage to serve on the Minnesota State Legislature, wrote the following about the tribal names: "The word is composed of ojib—pucker up—and abwe—to roast—and it means to roast till puckered up. . . . It is well authenticated by their traditions, and by the writings of their early white discoverers, that before they became acquainted with, and made use of fire arm and other European weapons of war, instead of their primitive bow and arrow and war club, their wars with other tribes were less deadly, and they were more accustomed to secure captives, whom under the uncontrolled feeling incited by aggravated wrong, and revenge for similar injuries, they tortured by fire in various ways.

"The name of abwenag—roasters—which the Ojibways have given to the Dakota . . . originated in their roasting their captives, and it is as likely that the word Ojibwa—to roast till puckered up—originated in the same manner. . . . The name of the tribe has been most commonly spelt, Chippeway, and is thus laid down in our different treaties with them, and officially used by our Government."

Warren, however, explained later in this book that the invented names of the woodland tribes do "not date far back. As a race or distinct people they denominated themselves Anishinaabeg. . . ."

Almost a century ago Frederic Baraga published the first dictionary of *anishinaabemowin*, the oral traditional language of the Anishinaabeg. Baraga, a priest and a latinist, interpreted *anishinaabemowin* according to written linguistic structures. The following words selected from *A Dictionary of the Otchipwe Language*, are quoted here to show the confusion in definitions of tribal names:

nind	the personal pronoun in anishinaabemowin
nind ojibwa	I write or mark on some object
ojibiigan	writing, writ, document
ojibiigewin	the act or art of writing
odishkwagami	Algonquin Indian
nind otchipwem	I speak the Chippewa language

nind otchipwew	I am a Chippewa Indian
otchipwemowin	the Chippewa language
anishinabe	human being, woman or child
anishinabemowin	the Indian language
anishinabe ijitwawin	Indian pagan religion
anishinabe nagamon	Indian song
anishinabe ogima	Indian agent
nind anishinabewadis	I have the Indian character
nind anishinabe bimadis	I live like an Indian
nind anishinabem	I speak Indian
nind anishinabew	I am a human being

Baraga defines *otchipwemowin* as the Chippewa language and *anishinaabemowin* as the Indian language and he defines Indian as Anishinaabe. There is, of course, no such language as the Indian language; the word *Indian* was invented and imposed on the tribes; it does not appear in the oral tradition of tribal cultures. The phonetic transcriptions of words from the Anishinaabe language, or *anishinaabemowin*, conform to the entries in *Ojibwewi-Ikidowinan* by Nichols and Nyholm, except where tribal words are quoted from printed texts or titles.

The tribal people named the Odjibwa, Otchipwe, Ojibway, Chippewa, and Chippeway in their oral traditional language still speak of themselves as the Anishinaabeg. Not only have certain tribal names been invented and ascribed in written form, but the personal names of tribal people have been changed and translated without cultural significance. When a tribal person is expected to understand several thousand years of tribal histories in the language of dominant societies, his identities are a dangerous burden. Two generations ago the Anishinaabeg, and other tribal cultures, were forbidden to speak their language and practice their religion. Now, in ethnographic monographs, tribal people are summoned to be proud of their invented Indian and Chippewa heritage as it appears in narrative histories. The cultural and political histories of the Anishinaabeg were written in a colonial language by those who invented the Indian, renamed the tribes, allotted the land, divided ancestries by geometric degrees of blood, and categorized identities on federal reservations.

"Since the original inhabitants of the Western Hemisphere neither called themselves by a single term nor understood themselves as a collectivity," Robert F. Berkhofer, Jr., writes in *The White Man's Indian: Images of the American Indian from Columbus to the Present*, "the idea and the image of the Indian must be a White conception. Native Americans were and are real, but the *Indian* was a White invention and still remains largely a White image, if not stereotype. . . . The first residents of the Americas

John Bad Boy and family,
White Earth Reservation,
about 1925. Photo courtesy
of Minnesota Historical
Society.

were by modern estimates divided into at least two thousand cultures
and more societies, practiced a multiplicity of customs and lifestyles, held
an enormous variety of values and beliefs, spoke numerous languages
mutually unintelligible to the many speakers, and did not conceive of
themselves as a single people. . . .

"By classifying all these many people as *Indians*, Whites categorized
the variety of cultures and societies as a single entity for the purposes
of description and analysis, thereby neglecting or playing down the social
and cultural diversity of Native Americans then—and now—for the convenience of simplified understanding. . . . Whether as a conception or
as a stereotype, however, the idea of the Indian has created a reality in
its own image as a result of the power of the Whites and the response
of Native Americans."

Kahgegagahbowh told his romantic white readers more than a century ago that "communities can be governed by the pure rules of Christianity, with less coercion than the laws of civilized nations, at present,
imposed upon their subjects. . . . A vast amount of evidence can be ad-

duced to prove that force has tended to brutalize rather than ennoble the Indian race. The more man is treated as a brother, the less demand for law . . . *the less law there is, the more will man be honored."*

DREAMS AND MUSIC
■

The sacred *miigis* shell of the Anishinaabeg spiritual world, a shell resembling the cowrie, arose from the eastern sea and moved with the seasons, it is told in the oral tradition, through the inland waters, guiding the Anishinaabeg through the sleeping sun of the woodland to *bawitig*, the long rapids in the river.

The Anishinaabeg tell stories that wisdom and the color of their skin were given to them from the sun reflecting on the sacred *miigis* shell during this long migration. Five hundred years ago, in mythic ceremonies, the *miigis* shell appeared in the sun for the last time at Mooningwanekaning, or Madeline Island, in Anishinaabe Gichigami, Lake Superior, the great sea of the Anishinaabeg.

The Anishinaabeg measured their lives in natural mythic time, through the circles of the sun and moon and human heart. The woodland tribes trailed the shores of Anishinaabe Gichigami to the hardwoods and swamps where families drew *ziinzibaakwad* from the maple trees in the spring, and gathered *manoomin*, or wild rice, in the autumn, and returned each winter to Mooningwanekaning. There the Anishinaabeg told stories of the summer past while the snow fell and the lakes froze.

In the seventeenth century, voyageurs and the first missionaries established a fur trading post on the island. The Anishinaabeg taught the traders and colonists how to endure the long woodland winters; less than half of the tribe survived a smallpox epidemic and other serious infections.

The Anishinaabeg and "other tribes among whom the blackrobes moved were tenacious of their ancient beliefs not because they were savages, as the Jesuits accused, but rather because their world view and ritual had been functional up until then," writes Calvin Martin in *Keepers of the Game: Indian-Animal Relations and the Fur Trade*. He asserts that diseases ruptured the sacred apposition between animals and the tribes, making possible a radical departure from traditional attitudes toward animals.

"The single most important deterrent to excessive hunting . . . was the fear of spiritual reprisal for indiscreet slaughter. . . . Nature, as conceived by traditional Ojibwa," Martin writes, "was a congeries of societies: every animal, fish, and plant species functioned in a society that was parallel in all respects" to human families. There were "keepers" of the game, or leaders of animal families. "The tribes could have attributed the causes of diseases to evil intrusion, punishment for the breech of a taboo: certain animals were malevolent and eager participation in the fur trade could have been a form of tribal vengeance and retaliation. The Indian, true to the behavioral environment in which he operated," Martin continues, "was convinced that the bear and the beaver . . . had conspired against man to destroy him. . . .

"Christian conversion must be understood, then, as an adjunct to disease. The two greatest killers were probably smallpox and plague, smallpox becoming endemic to the area by the mid-seventeenth century. Over the years these were joined by rickets, tuberculosis, syphilis, typhus, cholera, scarlet fever, and others—diseases which would sweep through a vulnerable native population in insidious clusters, decimating and demoralizing the victims."

Henry Dobyns has contributed important information to the understanding of tribal populations. In a recent critical bibliography, *Native American Historical Demography*, he writes that new estimates place the hemispheric tribal population at one hundred million at the time of the first white contact. Ten million of that total inhabited North America, ten times the estimates in popular histories; and about thirty million more tribal people lived in what is now Mexico.

"Native Americans achieved those densities during prehistoric times because they inhabited a relatively disease-free paradise and domesticated high-yield cereals and tubers," Dobyns writes. "Europeans destroyed that paradise—not intentionally, but simply because they carried Old World disease agents. Native Americans lacked immunities or resistance to Old World pathogens, and even lacked knowledge of nursing techniques for the care of the ill.

"Smallpox became the single most lethal disease Europeans carried to the New World. This contagion repeatedly spread through Native American peoples, killing a high proportion of susceptible individuals not immunized by surviving a previous epidemic."

William Denevan points out in *The Native Population of the Americas in 1492* that "most historians now agree that introduced disease was the major killer of New World Indians and seems to be the only way to explain the rapidity of decline in many areas. This is confirmed by hundreds of reports in the documentary record. Single epidemics reduced villages by half or more, and the people of many tribes were completely wiped out in a few decades. . . . The discovery of America was followed by possibly the greatest demographic disaster in the history of the world. And unlike past population crises in Europe and Asia from epidemics, wars, and climate, where full recovery did occur, the Indian population of America recovered only slowly, partially, and in highly modified form. . . . Many of those groups that have survived remain threatened with extinction for much the same reasons as in the sixteenth century: disease, inhumanity, misguided 'salvation,' and racial and cultural mixing to the point of non-recognition."✗

The passionate missionaries latinized the woodland dead and thundered through their epistles that the Anishinaabeg were mere children, one generation removed from savagism. Weakened from lethal pathogens, tribal families were bound to remember their introduction to civilization. While the discoverers learned the languages and humor of the woodland, the tribes were enmeshed in the predatory economics of the fur trade. The expanding interests of the trade, spurred on by the bourgeois demand for felt hats, drew tribal people to other fur posts in the woodland, a precursor of new sacrifices of the earth; beaver and the pelts from other animals were exchanged for firearms, diluted intoxicants, and material sundries. With rifles, the Anishinaabeg defeated the woodland Dakota and drove them from the lakes, which were rich with wild rice, and from the land, which later became valuable to white settlers.

> *moving forward and back*
> *from the woodland to the prairie*
> *dakota women*
> *weeping*
> *as they gather*
> *their wounded men*
> *the sound of their weeping*
> *comes back to us*

The fur trade and other colonial interests interposed economic anomalies between the intuitive rhythms of woodland life and the equipoise of the Anishinaabeg spiritual world. While the tribes were reluming their human unities with the earth, thousands of white settlers peddled their terminal creeds and procured the land with new laws and liens; the Anishinaabeg and other tribes were enslaved in the furies of discovery.

> *honoring your brave men*
> *like them*
> *believing in myself*

Tribal dreams and visions of the earth were broken by the marching cadence of colonial patriotism. Anishinaabeg orators of the *maang*, or loon, families, legions of the *makwa*, or bear, and the people of the *amik*, or beaver, were categorized, removed, and segregated from their woodland life and religion while the voices of the conquerors clanged with the technical sounds of freedom.

> *brave warriors*
> *where have you gone*
> *ho kwi ho ho*

Frederick Turner, in *Beyond Geography: The Western Spirit Against the Wilderness*, writes that the sacred tribal attachment to the earth "amounted to a different kind of possession than the whites were prepared to understand as they looked about these spaces and found them empty of visible marks of tenancy. . . . To them the lands were satanic rather than sacred, and the traders and their employees could tolerate the wilderness only in the hope that eventually they could make enough money to leave it behind and return to civilization to live like humans. So they would grimly push out into the woods beyond the farthest reach of civilization. . . . Here they would establish a post and make it known that they stood ready to supply the needs of the resident tribes in return for pelts taken in trapping and hunting. . . . Here again we encounter the clash between history and myth, with the whites, driven to enormous technological ingenuity, producing a vast array of seductive items for peoples of the globe whose spiritual contentments had kept their own technologies at comparatively simple levels. . . . We know now that there has been no people on earth capable of resisting this seduction, for none has been able to see the hidden and devious byways that lead inevitably from the consumption of the new luxuries to the destruction of the myths that give life its meaning."

The Anishinaabeg did not have written histories; their world views were not linear narratives that started and stopped in manifest binaries. The tribal past lived as an event in visual memories and oratorical gestures; woodland identities turned on dreams and visions. Keeshkemun, a tribal elder, told the colonial officers that he was a bird, "if you wish to know me you must seek me in the clouds." Keeshkemun responded with a dream song when the officers asked him to explain his position in the territorial wars.

Tribal leaders were dreamers and orators, speaking in visual metaphors as if the past were a state of being in the telling. Tribal words have power in the oral tradition, the sounds express the spiritual energies of woodland lives. The Anishinaabeg did not borrow words from other languages to speak about their own dreams and lived experiences in the woodland. The words the woodland tribes spoke were connected to the place the words were spoken. The poetic images were held, for some tribal families, in song pictures and in the rhythms of visions and dreams in

Anishinaabe family on the
shore of Cass Lake, about
1900. Photo courtesy of
Minnesota Historical Society.

music: timeless and natural patterns of seeing and knowing the energies of the earth. The Anishinaabeg drew pictures that reminded them of ideas, visions, and dreams, that were tribal connections to the earth. These song pictures, especially those of the Midewiwin, or the Grand Medicine Society, were incised on the soft inner bark of the birch tree. These birch scrolls of pictomyths and sacred songs are taught and understood only by members of the Midewiwin, who believe that music and the knowledge and use of herbal medicine extend human life.

Frances Densmore lived at White Earth, Leech Lake, Red Lake, and other reservations, where she recorded Anishinaabeg songs on wax cylinders. The songs she recorded were later transcribed and published, about the turn of the last century, by the Smithsonian Institution, Bureau of American Ethnology, with literal translations and explanatory notes obtained from the individual tribal singers.

Densmore wrote that the Anishinaabeg had no songs that were the "exclusive property of families or clans . . . a young man may learn his father's songs . . . but he does not inherit the right to sing such songs, nor does his father force him to learn them. . . .

"The melody is evidently considered more important than the words . . . the idea is the important thing, and this is firmly connected with the melody in the minds" of the Anishinaabeg singers. The singer had a characteristic wavering tone of voice. The singer sang alone, accompanied by the sound of a drum or rattle. The other musical instrument used by the Anishinaabeg was the flute.

In *The Winged Serpent*, Margot Astrov writes that "rhythm is the repetition of units that are either similar or contrasting." Rhythm may have a physiological basis that "corresponds to certain physiological processes, as for instance the contraction and expansion of the respiratory organs, the pulsating of the blood, the beating of the heart. But this drive that forces man to express himself in rhythmic patterns has its ultimate source in psychic need . . . the need of spiritual ingestion and proper organization of all the multiform perceptions and impressions rushing forever upon the individual from without and within."

The images in the songs of tribal people are the products of "cosmic feeling," writes Nellie Barnes in *American Indian Verse*, published more than sixty years ago. "The Indian's observations, esthetic sense, and vigor of thought shape the image to his need—a direct picture, a comparison or a contrast."

Thomas Vennum, in his introduction to *Chippewa Music* by Frances Densmore, writes that "we are particularly indebted to her for collecting the *oldest* songs of the tribe, thereby rescuing them from certain oblivion. It is remarkable that she was able to record as much of the sacred repertoire as she did. The Chippewa singers were as reluctant as those of other tribes to give up their music . . . despite assurances that their voices would be forever preserved. . . ." One tribal singer was ostracized from the Midewiwin lodge because he disclosed religious secrets and allowed sacred songs to be recorded. Vennum asserts that the "substance of Chippewa music has not been radically affected and continues to be virtually uninfluenced by Western Music. Singers use many of the same vocal techniques, tonal patterns, and song forms that one hears" on the original wax cylinder recordings.

ANTHROPOLOGICAL AND HISTORICAL INVENTIONS
■

Traditional tribal people imagine their social patterns and places on the earth, whereas anthropologists and historians invent tribal cultures and end mythic time. The differences between tribal imagination and social scientific invention are determined in world views: imagination is a state of being, a measure of personal courage; the invention of cultures is a material achievement through objective methodologies. To imagine the world is to be in the world; to invent the world with academic predications is to separate human experiences from the world, a secular transcendence and denial of chance and mortalities.

Roy Wagner, in *The Invention of Culture*, argues that "anthropology exists through the idea of culture," which is an invention. "The study of culture *is* culture. . . . The study of culture is in fact *our* culture; it operates through our forms, creates in our terms, borrows our words and concepts for its meanings, and re-creates us through our efforts." Modern established cultures, and ideological pastiche cultures, tame and temper nature and tribal mythic imagination through institutions and entertainment. Truculence, even intense human passion, for example, is denied in common interaction, but brutal violence is allowed as a form of passive entertainment in motion pictures. The dominant collective culture, Wagner asserts, "is a vast accumulation of material and spiritual achievements and resources stemming from the conquest of nature and necessary to the continuance of this effort."

The Anishinaabeg have been invented by ethnocentric methodologists who wear the professional cloaks of missionaries, ethnologists, anthropologists, and historians. From Henry Rowe Schoolcraft to Edmund Jefferson Danziger the Anishinaabeg have been invented, separated from their imaginative recollections, which has allowed a material and linguistic colonization of tribal families.

For example, in the foreword to *Anishinabe: 6 Studies on Modern Chip-*

pewa, a collation of ethnographic research, Ruth Landes writes that the tribal people in this book "are zestful and wicked survivors, extremely alert to the possibilities of an ungenerous environment. Their wit is cruel and startling to the white middle-class outsider, at whom it is often directed. Their celebrated pursuit of spiritual protectors, through visions induced deliberately by starvation and thirst, has produced fierce and remarkable sorcerers."

With that invention and dubious preamble by a renowned anthropologist, one would expect an unusual tribal adventure in the data wilderness of the new world, trickeries at least; but the contents of this book, a coarse collection of graduate theses on acculturation, politics, wild rice, peyote, and powwows, are cast in familiar untribal methodologies. No sorcerer could survive the insipid tabulations. Meanwhile, there are tribal people in cities and on reservations who must resist data colonization, social science categorization, and shovel out the academic dossier to free their dreams and families.

The studies in this book, as in numerous other books on tribal cultures, are inventions not based on lived experiences. "A Peyote Community in Northern Minnesota," by Barbara Jackson, for example, is an invitation to an unusual experience, but behind the title is a rather dull description of a material place, not a psychic or spiritual event, which includes two full pages of floor plans for village houses. "The privies are small, simple, unpainted wood structures," Jackson writes, "located in the brush behind the houses they serve."

The chapter written by Gretel Pelto, "Chippewa People and Politics in a Reservation Town," holds more historical and ethnographic information than the other studies. The town she writes about, Cass Lake on the Leech Lake Reservation, which she fictionalizes as James Lake on the Broken Reed Reservation, is where racial violence toward tribal people was common; meanwhile, she folds cultures from questionnaires. "There has been little disagreement," Pelto writes, "among the various researchers about the behavior picture at the present time or in the distant past; the arguments have centered around the question of whether this is a continuous or a discontinuous phenomenon."

J. Anthony Paredes, in the concluding chapter, raises the question of conceptualizing distinct tribal entities in present dominant cultures. "Many Chippewa know little of native languages and lore," he writes; "in much of their daily behavior they differ little from their white neighbors." Paredes asserts that the tribal people he studied "no longer constitute a tribal culture in the anthropological sense," which, in an ironic manner, is a liberation from theoretical categories. "Besides powwows,

Anishinaabeg family, about
1905. Photo courtesy of
Minnesota Historical Society.

ricing, and wakes," he continues, "numerous other elements of more or
less traditional Chippewa culture—language, supernatural beliefs, oral
literature, and handicrafts—are still to be found among the modern Chippewa. However, they are not nearly so widespread among the Chippewa

as is participation in ricing, powwows, and wakes. Furthermore, the opportunities for social expression of these other beliefs and behaviors are limited, since they tend to be individual rather than group traits. In contrast, powwows, ricing, and wakes provide opportunities for participation in Indian activities regardless of whether an individual can speak Chippewa, believes in grand medicine, or can tan a deer hide."

The Chippewa of Lake Superior by Edmund Jefferson Danziger, a more recent example of the invention of the Anishinaabeg, is a linear historical thesis on the impact of three centuries of European and American societies on woodland tribal cultures. No trickeries or sorcerers here, either; the tribal people on these pages appear more like victims of civilization than survivors.

"In the winter of their lives," Danziger writes about the traditional culture he invents, "the old warriors and women sat crosslegged in snow covered wigwams, surrounded by children and grandchildren. Much respect and attention was bestowed upon them. . . . When their hearts beat no more families mourned the loss." Five chapters later, from romantic wigwam scenes to unemotional data on the fur trade, treaties, and reservations, we learn that "thousands of woodland hunters and their families abandoned traditional semi-nomadic ways. . . . The portable birch-bark wigwams gave way to one-room log or frame cabins. . . . Tubercular red men, coughing away in smoke-filled rooms, must have doubted the virtues of reservation life."

Danziger invents a romantic tribal culture and then he compares ersatz families from a data culture to complete a simple thesis that the impact of other cultures has been adverse. Such assumptions prevail in historical literature, but the way the axiom tumbles in academic print marks a vast distance between racial sensitivities and arrogance. The author borrows what appears to be random data from selected populations to reach improper conclusions; as a result, tribal people appear as victims in a colonial dramalogue.

Danziger assumes that tribal hunters in the fur trade "modified their traditional economic pursuits more readily than their religious practices and beliefs." In conclusion, however, he states that "only a handful of tribesmen on each reservation practice the old ways of living," but allows that the "resistant remnants of a shattered culture have assumed great importance." To reach this resolution the author studied unrelated populations, compared abstract families with individuals, and generalized demographic data from diverse times and places. For example, the author borrows information from alcoholism studies that show that seven years ago in Minnesota, Indian drinking reached "epidemic proportions." He does not disclose the number of persons studied or the methods of research behind this racial assumption—an apparent data distortion of a complex human problem.

The best stories about the tribal people invented in these studies must have been reserved for telling at professional academic conferences. Tricksters and the "zestful and wicked survivors" familiar to most people who have shared tribal humor are not to be found in these two books.

WOODLAND RESERVATIONS

■

The Minnesota Chippewa Tribe is a federation of representative governments on six reservations in the state. These reservations, White Earth, Leech Lake, Mille Lacs, Nett Lake, Fond du Lac, and Grand Portage, were established by several treaties with the federal government. The Red Lake Reservation, the seventh reservation in the state, is original tribal land that has never been ceded to the federal government. The Red Lake Anishinaabeg were not moved from one place to another; the members of the reservation hold in common the title to their land. Title to tribal land on the other six reservations, however, was held in trust and then allotted to individual tribal members; the federal government sold the land not allotted. Although the number of acres of tribal land has diminished, the boundaries of the treaties have remained the same. Civil agreements and various court decisions over tribal rights to hunt and fish have been based on the boundaries established in treaties rather than on the actual land tribal people or tribal governments now own or lease.

Before the federal government created a representative system of government on the six reservations, the Anishinaabeg were organized in large families with hereditary leaders. Political affiliation was established through marriages, and through other agreements between families. The six reservations are now governed by elected tribal business committees, with the assistance and interference of the United States Department of the Interior and the Bureau of Indian Affairs. Two elected members from each reservation business committee serve on the Minnesota Chippewa Tribal Executive Committee, which supervises tribal land use and general business for all six reservations. Civil and criminal laws and policies are enforced by county, and in some cases municipal, state, and federal governments, with the exception of jurisdiction over hunting and fishing rights on the White Earth and Leech Lake reservations, where the tribal executive committees have established and maintain conservation codes

Sam Davis and family,
Onamia, about 1909. Photo
courtesy of Minnesota
Historical Society.

and policies of enforcement. The federal courts in the past decade have
upheld tribal claims for control of reservation resources; at the same time,
each reservation must negotiate a unique agreement with the state government for institutional control of these rights.

The Anishinaabeg have been divided by colonial, national, territorial,
and state claims. Certain rights have been restored to tribal communities
according to the interests of local governments, but in spite of these divi-
sions, there exists a sense of common tribal consciousness. Anishinaabeg
people live on provincial reserves in Ontario and Manitoba and on reservations in Minnesota, Wisconsin, Michigan, and North Dakota.

The White Earth Reservation is located in the northwestern part of
the state. Only eight percent of the original treaty land established by
the federal government in 1867 is now owned by tribal people. More than
two thousand Anishinaabeg live on the reservation in several communities, including Pine Point, Ponsford, White Earth village, Beaulieu,
and Naytahwaush.

The Leech Lake Reservation is located in the north central part of the
state. Only about twenty percent of the original treaty land is now owned

by tribal people. The reservation was established in 1855. The Anishinaabeg population is estimated to be close to three thousand, located in Cass Lake, Onigum, Squaw Lake, Bena, Ball Club, Inger, Federal Dam, Deer River, and other communities.

The Nett Lake Reservation is located near the northern border of the state. About forty percent of the original treaty land established by the federal government in 1866 is now owned by tribal people. Less than one thousand Anishinaabeg live on the reservation and in the nearby communities of Vermilion Lake and Tower.

The Fond du Lac Reservation is located about twenty miles west of Duluth. More than half of the original treaty land established in 1854 is now owned by tribal people. About seven hundred Anishinaabeg live on the reservation and in the communities of Cloquet and Sawyer, close to the reservation boundaries.

The Mille Lacs Reservation is located in the central part of the state. The reservation was established in treaties by those Anishinaabeg who refused to remove to the other reservations in the state. About six hundred tribal people live in the communities of Onamia, Garrison, Vineland, and Isle.

The Grand Portage Reservation is located on the shores of Lake Superior in the northeastern corner of the state. Close to eighty percent, the most of any ceded reservation in the state, of the original treaty land established by the federal government in 1854 is now owned by tribal people. Several hundred Anishinaabeg live on this scenic reservation in the community of Grand Portage and about one hundred reservation members live in the town of Grand Marais.

The Red Lake Reservation is located in the northwestern part of the state. The land on the reservation has never been ceded or resettled in treaties with the federal government, with the exception of tribal land holdings on the Northwest Angle. Close to three thousand Anishinaabeg live on the reservation in the communities of Red Lake, Redby, and Ponemah, one of the most traditional tribal communities in the state. About fifty years ago, the people on the reservation were the first to organize under a written constitution by a council of hereditary leaders. The reservation is now governed by a council of eleven members elected by the enrolled members of the reservation to serve four-year terms.

Because the reservation land has never been ceded to the federal government, the tribe maintains limited criminal and civil jurisdiction over residents on the reservation. Neither the land nor the tribal people on the reservation have been held in trust to the federal government. Red Lake is a distinct place: the reservation issues automobile license plates to residents. The hereditary leaders on the reservation still serve in an

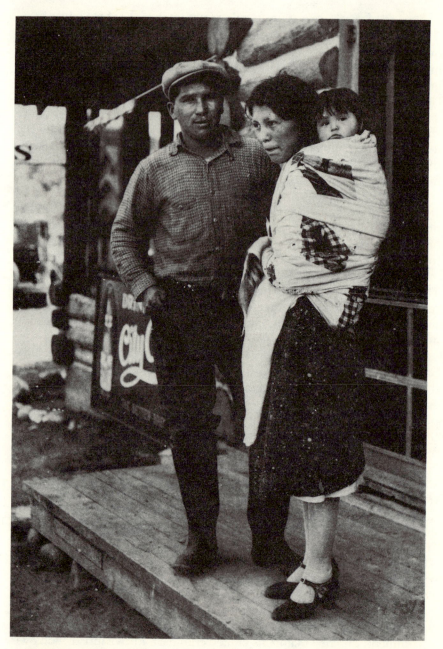

Tom and Mary Wind and
their child in front of
Miller's Tea Room Store,
Wigwam Bay, Mille Lacs,
about 1925. Photo courtesy
of Minnesota Historical
Society.

advisory capacity to the elected tribal council. There are tribal police officers and tribal courts; and the public school on the reservation is operated as an independent district. On the other six reservations under the Minnesota Chippewa Tribal Executive Committee, Anishinaabeg students attend high school in white communities near each reservation.

The estimated number of tribal people who live in urban areas in the state varies from between ten and twenty thousand. According to recent census studies, urban tribal populations now equal or exceed the number of tribal people who live on reservations. Census enumerations underestimate actual tribal populations, but even so, the various estimates of urban populations reflect the needs of tribal communities, the ideologies and ambitions of individuals who present demographic data in proposals for state and federal funds. Fifteen thousand is a reasonable estimate of the number of Anishinaabeg living in Minneapolis and Saint Paul, and the surrounding metropolitan area. For several decades tribal people have argued that the largest reservation is in Minneapolis and Saint Paul. The primary tribal group there is Anishinaabe, whereas in other urban areas, there is a much more diverse tribal population. Radical tribal leaders have demanded equal services and programs from federal agencies—services and entitlements that have been, in the recent past, limited to tribal people living on or near reservations recognized by the federal government. Although the recognized reservation population has decreased in the past decade, the funds allocated to reservations have increased.

Five Anishinaabeg reservations are in Wisconsin. The federal government signed treaties more than a century ago establishing the Bad River, Red Cliff, Lac du Flambeau, Lac Courte Oreille, and Sokaogon-Mole Lake reservations. Since the original treaties were signed, collective tribal land and individual allotments on these five reservations have been reduced in some areas by more than half.

The Bad River Reservation in northern Wisconsin near Lake Superior is the largest reservation in the state. About four hundred Anishinaabeg live in Odanah, a small village on the reservation.

The Red Cliff Reservation is located on the northernmost point of Wisconsin, near the town of Bayfield, across from historical Madeline Island on the shores of Lake Superior. Several hundred Anishinaabeg live on this beautiful reservation and another hundred tribal people live in and around white communities in the area.

The Lac du Flambeau Reservation is located in the northern part of the state. About nine hundred Anishinaabeg live on the reservation.

The Lac Courte Oreille Reservation is located in the northwestern part of the state near Hayward. About eight hundred Anishinaabeg live on the reservation in the communities of Reserve, and New Post, Wisconsin.

The Sokaogon-Mole Lake Reservation, the smallest of all the reservations, is located in the northeastern portion of the state. Less than two hundred Anishinaabeg live on the reservation in the community of Mole Lake.

SHADOWS AT LA POINTE

∎

*I believe that all narration, even
that of a very ordinary event, is
an extension of the stories told by
the great myths that explain how
this world came into being and
how our condition has come to be
as we know it today. I think that
an interest in narration is part of
our mode of being in the world.
. . . And man will never be able
to do without listening to stories.*
Mircea Eliade,
Ordeal by Labyrinth

∎

This morning the lake is clear and calm.

Last night a cold wind washed slivers of ice clear over the beach, the end of a winter to remember. Now, the pale green becomes blue on the horizon. Spring opens in the birch, a meadow moves in the wind. The trees thicken down to the water, an invitation to follow the sun over the old fur trade post to a new world of adventures.

We are late for school.

The slivers of ice that marked the first cattails melt. The sun is warmer on our cheeks. We turn from side to side, new wild flowers. In the distance a thin banner of smoke rises from the first steamer of the season.

We wait on the beach near the dock.

The sand is smooth and cold under our fingers.

MARGARET CADOTTE

ANGELICK FRONSWA

In large block letters we print our names down to the cold water rim, our last names hold back the flood. We are certain that the people who come here on the steamer to visit this island will notice our names and remember that we were here first and late for school. We will be remembered in the future because we boarded the first steamer that followed the sun in our dreams. Someone will tell stories that we were the first mixedbloods on the island, a new people on the earth, and that our names would last forever because we learned how to read and write in a mission school.

Last week when we were late for school, we heard the old men tell stories about the hard winters on the island in the past, a sure message that one more winter had ended. We sat near the old woodstove in the American Fur Company store, painted bright red outside, and listened to the men catch their words in their wrinkled hands. We listened to stories about hard times, adventures on the trail, white men in the bush, and disasters on the lake. The fur trade had changed from the old days remembered in the stories when there were more animals. The market and the animals moved to a new place on the earth; the animals in tribal dreams were weakened by white politics, diseases, competition, and new fashions, but there are hundreds of barrels of fish and corn stored from the last season to feed a population of more than six hundred people. The men in the fur business, the missionaries and their wives, about fifteen people on the island, were white. The rest were tribal people, and more than half were mixedblood families.

We remembered the stories:

Eliza Morrison, mixedblood wife of the hunter and trader John Morrison, was born in November 1837 at La Pointe on Madeline Island. "As I remember," she writes in an autobiographical letter, "there used to be thirty seven houses on the flats, all of them made of round logs roofed with cedar bark.

"My uncle built a house alongside of ours. For a period of thirty years he was one of those who traded with the Chippewas off to the north and west. They used to get goods from the Company to go out and establish their posts during the winter. They would be gone eight months from home each year and would return quite late in the spring. They used dogs, when they had them. My uncle told me that the Indians would not sell dogs, but they would hire them out to those who were trading with the Indians. The dogs were very large. I used to see some of them brought in. They were yellow, had long hair, and looked like wolves.

"When I was a girl the Chippewas used to come to La Pointe to be paid off by the government. To my knowledge the largest payment made was eighteen dollars a head. Thousands of Indians came to the island at one time for pay. I used to be very afraid of them. Our folks used to keep us from school while payments were made."

Later, she and her husband moved to Spider Lake near Iron River, Wisconsin, deep in the woodland. She wrote about the hard winters and construction of the first railroad in the area. "My husband feared that we would have to go without bread before spring. . . ." Her husband and eldest son had to leave to find food. "I made up my mind that if they were not back by the time our provisions were consumed I would first kill the chickens to keep my children from starving. . . . When I thought about those hard times my grandmother had, I wondered what would happen to my children and me should my husband and boy fail to get through to Ashland. . . . We had only enough grub for two more meals, small ones at that," when they returned with provisions.

"When the snow got too deep for hunting, my husband began tanning deerskins to have them ready to sell. We both took time to teach our boys to read. We had some friends who would send us books.

"I would say it is hard for me to write a history of my forest life in English. My husband and I would talk to one another in Chippewa, but to our children we spoke in English as much as we could. My husband had a chance to go to school to learn to read and write. He can write in English and in Chippewa if necessary, and he can also talk French when it comes to that. . . . Thirty years ago, about two out of every ten Indians could speak English. Now three-fourths of them can speak English," she remembers from the turn of the century, when she first wrote about her experiences, "but when I see their complexion I feel like using my native language to talk with them. They are pretty well civilized, but there are some who still follow the medicine dance, the pen names, and other old habits.

"The Indians in this vicinity are selling the timber off their allotments. This enables them to live in good houses. Not one family lives in a wigwam anymore. There is a big sawmill here where they can buy lumber. Some have large gardens and sell vegetables to the whites. They hunt in the fall and gather wild rice. And it is a great place for hunting ducks in the spring and in the fall.

"I have nothing more to write. I might say that I have almost consumed the history of my life. Well, I believe this is the end of my story." Eliza died at age eighty-three.

Provident people were seldom without food on the island, we were told time and time again in school. The old tribal mixedbloods remembered that gospel, the one about being civilized, in their slowest stories at the fire. The men turned one to the other, like ceremonial birds around the stove, and winked, pulled at their ears, winked more, smiled some, and then looked down in silence at the stove. The stove seemed human, a listener: the fire cracked on, a wind-checked side of white pine inside, while the old men waited for the first steamer of the season to reach the dock.

We listened to more stories:

One man pulled at his beard and told about the little people on the island. He crouched forward in his chair and measured with his slender hands, floor to nose, "those little fellows were no more than three feet, not one of them could see over the packs they carried with a tumpline across their foreheads.

"These little people were covered with tattoos, one mark for all the fur posts between Montreal and Fort Pierre, and they drank dark rum mixed with wine on the trail," the old man said as he leaned back in his chair and aimed his long finger past his ear, behind him, toward the east. The visitors followed the direction of his finger. "Back there, clear across the widest angle of the lake you can smell those little pork eaters coming upwind a week ahead in a rain storm . . . the smell of pork moves quicker than the eye of a crow."

A stout mixedblood under a wide fur hat told about the time when government agents from the East sent saddles to the woodland, because they thought that all tribal people must ride horses. "A thumb rider in a wild east show shipped us a dozen saddles, so as, no doubt, we could catch rabbits from above.

"One of the missionaries found two horses and tried to teach us to ride," said the old trapper. He never changed his focus from the base of the stove as he spoke. He seemed to growl when he spoke, and between phrases, even single words at times, he ground his front teeth together. "The best we could do was cut four holes in a canoe and teach the horses to paddle."

Then a wizened old mixedblood with a smart smile, like a mongrel on a trap line, clapped his hands, pulled up his sleeves to reveal dozens of tattoos dedicated to his wives. "And then some," he added, and all the old men laughed around the stove in the American Fur Company store. When he turned down his sleeves his face turned sallow. He looked into the fire and told about the time he was mentioned in a printed book.

"Thomas Loraine McKenney came through these parts on his tour to the lakes," the mixedblood said as he leaned forward in his chair, the hard wooden chair creaked. The old men and visitors were silent. The fire snapped. "We called the place Michael's Island then, and this McKenney was a demanding fellow with swift eyes and a nervous hand, he must have come from a place where people salute too much. . . . Anyway, he wrote about an old fisherman on the island, sixty-nine years of age, and active as a boy," the old man remembered. He reached into his inside shirt pocket and removed a folded sheet of paper, a page from a book. "Here is what he wrote," the old man said as he began to read. The visitors who had arrived that morning on the steamer shifted their feet on the rough wooden floor, impressed that the old mixedblood could read, and fine print at that.

"His pulse beats only twenty-five strokes in a minute. On his legs, and arms, and breast are tattooed the marks of superiority in his profession, which had been that of a voyageur, and it seems he excelled in carrying packages across the portages, both on account of their weight and the celerity of his movement. . . . On questioning him as to his former life, he said with a slap of the hands, 'he had been the greatest man in the Northwest.' "

"That man," said the old mixedblood as he folded with care the book page and returned it to his pocket, "is me, the greatest man in the Northwest." He opened his shirt and there beneath the thin strands of white hair on his chest, like a sleet storm, was a faded sunset scene on a lake with two crude loons and a canoe.

The third old mixedblood at the American Fur Company store that morning told true stories about the tall people who came from the East. The tall people, he explained to the visitors, never trusted the little people because some little people pretended to be tall people, mocked the tall people in their dances. Tall people never pretend to be little, no matter how far their fortunes fall. Tall people are white, educated, they march and give orders, sweat in dark clothes, and hold pet birds in house cages. The little people are mixedbloods who wear bright colors, dance and dream out of time, trick their friends, animals and birds, in good humor.

"Henry Rowe Schoolcraft was a tall person," the old mixedblood revealed. "He was more than eight feet tall in the cold, even when he slouched. The little people, the pork eaters, had to stand on a trunk or a fence rail to speak in similar space. Schoolcraft was a geologist, a government agent, treaty commissioner, who explored the sacred copper regions of the tribes with Lewis Cass, the territory governor of Michigan.

"Schoolcraft believes he found the sacred copper back on the Ontonogan River but he was mistaken. The shamans planted a chunk of mined copper there; the explorer thought that he had discovered more than the next white man, which made him taller. With the copper find he sprouted an additional inch back East, an inch less in the tribe. He remained the same height when he tried to change the name of this place to Virginia Island. Madeline, the mixedblood wife of Michel Cadotte, remained the favorite name, the place name on the maps.

"He also asked tribal people, even a few mixedbloods, where to find the source of the Mississippi River. He asked his way and then revealed his discoveries back East. He lost three inches there, gained one back in humor, but he took on six more inches back East for the river find. He was a giant then, and it was time to find a mixedblood wife from the wilderness. He did just that, in the daughter of John Johnson, the fur trader from La Pointe. Johnson, who was Irish, married the daughter of Waubojeeg, or Chief White Fisher.

"Schoolcraft gained back a few inches with his marriage, but lost more than a foot when he became an expert on the 'red race' and when he invented the 'Algic tribes,' as he called us out here. This copper hunter learned all he knew about tribal people from his mixedblood relatives, but he gives them no credit for his discoveries.

"When Schoolcraft was the United States Indian agent at Mackinac he came to the island for another visit. We saw him down at the dock, eight to nine feet tall, white people all stood on stools and stilts to shake his enormous hand, as if his hand was a healing animal from a strange place.

"When the tall man died," said the old man in a loud voice to hold the ears of the visitors, "the tribe made a grave house for him about four feet long and put it out behind the mission in the weeds, but back East, we were told, the tall man was buried in a ten foot coffin. . . . Some tell that his coffin is two feet longer since his death, and still growing. . . . The grave house out here has become a bird nest, and even smaller."

The visitors soon departed from the store, ears filled, to conduct their business with the traders, the coopers, and the brownstone cutters, before the steamer departed from the island. Later, the visitors learned that they left the store too soon and missed the best stories about tall people by the old mixedblood with the tattoos. While he told his stories he did a striptease around the stove, exposed all his tattoos but three.

"The second time we heard that tall man with the nervous hands, Thomas Loraine McKenney, that talk and walk man, was out at the American Fur Company post at Fond du Lac," said the mixedblood as he danced in slow motions around the fire. "McKenney was twelve feet tall there, three feet taller than he was when he discovered and wrote about me on the island, twelve feet tall no less; we knew this because the soldiers packed him there flat in a *canot du nord* with room enough for a brass band. Flags and his wild red hair, red as the outside of this store, waved from shore to shore.

"When a man speaks from three sides of his mouth at once, a special number in the government service," said the mixedblood as he danced, "you know he is twelve feet tall and from the East because the little people are three feet tall and it took two of them, one on top of the other, to even shake his hand.

"That twelve foot red said from one side of his mouth that we were his equals, from another side he told us we were children, and from the third side of his mouth he said we were savages. No telling how a mixedblood would be parted in his mouth.

"We never forgot the old red threat and what he said and wrote about the tribes," said the little mixedblood who had removed his coat and shirt to reveal a second time the scenic tattoo on his chest.

McKenney and Governor Lewis Cass, who was much taller than the red one, told us that we were "the worst clad and the most wretched body of Indians" that he ever met with. . . . He said we were "wandering savages who inhabit the sterile and unhospitable shores of the northern lakes . . . the most miserable and degraded of the native tribes. . . . They have little ambition and few ideas. . . ," which was what we wanted the tall people in the government to think about us because when the tall ones admire a tribe, the people become pets and lose their land, their shadows, and their humor.

"We laughed and laughed and danced and dreamed about the tall ones in white water, too tall to fit in their canoes," chanted the old mixedblood as he danced. He did not remove his trousers, but he did fold up the legs to reveal several tattoos in honor of his wives and children and fur post encounters with the tall people. "The canoes turn and the tall logs shoot the rapids, turn wide, dam the rivers, and stop the white water . . . for a time."

"The tall red one spoke to us at Fond du Lac, his words rolled like logs in white water, he demanded that we produce the murderers of four white people," said the mixedblood who stopped his dance and stood erect about four feet tall near the stove. "So we did that, we named four tribal people, and hundreds more who had been murdered by white soldiers and settlers . . . we danced in the dark and named the dead until morning.

"McKenney was not pleased with us, and as he spoke he got smaller and smaller, his lips rolled at a great distance when he told us that 'this is not a thing to pass away like a cloud,' so we named more dead and danced for all those who died at the hands of the tall people. 'If they are not surrendered then,' the tall red one continued, 'destruction will fall on your women and children. Your father will put out his strong arm. Go, and think of it. Nothing will satisfy us but this.'

"We danced until he disappeared in the distance, a small animal on the run, too small to notice, then in a swarm of transparent flies he vanished," the old mixedblood concluded as he resumed his dance around the stove. Animals and dream figures, faces from the little people in his past, sagged and shivered on the calves of his thin legs.

Richard Drinnon, in *Facing West: The Metaphysics of Indian-Hating and Empire-Building*, writes about the arrival of Colonel Thomas McKenney, who was "tall and had a military carriage and a shock of red hair," and the other white commissioners at the American Fur Company post at Fond du Lac on July 28, 1826: The expedition, a squadron of barges and canoes which contained a detachment of soldiers, a company band, and staff assistants, "stretched out over a quarter mile, all in order, and 'all with flags flying, and martial music,' " according to the memoirs of the commissioner. "Ashore the troops drilled each morning and were inspected by General Cass and Colonel McKenney, with the latter in his militia uniform. . . ."

McKenney, with more on his mind than land and treaties, demanded that the tribe "produce the alleged murderers of four whites. 'It is a serious matter,' he declared, and unless they obeyed 'you will be visited with your great father's heaviest displeasure. No trader shall visit you — not a pound of tobacco, nor a yard of cloth, shall go into your country. This is not a thing to pass away like a cloud.' Spokesmen for the band under suspicion replied it was difficult to speak for their absent tribesmen."

The man who threatened the tribe, Drinnon writes, "is perhaps better described as high-handed rather than high-minded. . . . McKenney confidently expected the destruction of tribal cultures. . . . He severed the family connections of his 'little Indians,' used mission schools to batter tribal relations, and by stripping away native languages sought to cut off all ties between generations." McKenney, who was celebrated by some as a champion of tribal reform, was appointed as the head of the new Bureau of Indian Affairs, which was then under the War Department.

We were late for school:

Abigail Spooner was our teacher at the first mission school on Madeline Island. She had a voice that hurt on a spring afternoon, but she worked ever so hard to teach us how to read and write. We were mixedbloods, halfbreeds, neither here nor there to some. Abba, as she was known to friends and families on the island, promised that we could establish in the wilderness a new civilization with books. We had some books, not many, and an occasional magazine passed from house to house, which we shelved in a special place in the corner of the schoolroom. The other books on the island were owned by Lyman Marcus Warren and Truman Warren. The brothers were married to Mary and Charlotte Cadotte, the mixedblood daughters of Michel Cadotte, who was an educated man and was once the factor at the fur post. These families, educated in the east with the tall people, were important; we did not ask to borrow their books to make *our* civilization.

Abba said, "if not now, then at the right time in heaven, the last and perfect civilization for those who believe and are righteous." We believed her then, but most of the time we found real evidence of the civilized world down at the store and at the American Fur Company dock when the steamers arrived with mail, supplies, and visitors.

"The girls with bead pantalets, porcupine moccasins, new blue broadcloth shawls, plaited hair and clean faces looked almost good enough to kiss," noted Charles Penny, who had accompanied the geologist Douglass Houghton on an expedition in search of copper. He visited the island and admired the mixedblood and tribal women of all ages.

Sherman Hall, the superintendent of the school at La Pointe, wrote a letter to a government agent that the teachers have continued their "labors as usual, endeavoring to instruct all who were willing to receive instruction from us, in the duties and doctrines of the Christian religion, and in letters. . . .

"The school during the year has numbered sixty-five different scholars, forty-three males, and twenty-two females. It has been kept in operation regularly during the year, except the usual vacations. . . . The proficiency of the scholars who have been regular attendants is very satisfactory. The branches taught have been spelling, reading, writing, arithmetic, geography and composition. The scholars are taught in the Ojibwa and English languages. The schools are open and free to all who choose to avail themselves of their privileges, no charge being made for books or other expenses. During the past year the Ojibwa and English spelling book, mentioned in my last report as being nearly ready for use, has been introduced into the schools, and used, it is believed, with good effect."

Sherman Hall was a Presbyterian who dedicated his time to the conversion of the tribes, even the mixedbloods. He arrived on the island with his wife and a tribal woman who was once married to a fur trader. Reverend Hall started the mission and the school, and the tribal woman served as his interpreter.

This was not as simple as it might appear, because most of the mixedblood families and the children in the school, like us, were Roman Catholic. This seemed to trouble Reverend Sherman more than the tribal ceremonial dances on the island. He was, at times, critical of Catholics, and once or twice we were released from school to receive our religious instruction. He complained in a letter to his father, who lived back East, that the boatmen and laborers in the fur trade, who were, for the most part, Canadian French and Catholic, "may be as wicked as they choose; the priest can pardon all their sins when they go to Mackinac next year. He will do it, if they pay him a few shillings. I have more fears that the Catholics will cause us difficulties, than the Indians will."

Reverend Hall and his wife were separated from their culture and families in the East. The two of them seemed to be lost, without shadows, with no humor to throw at the weather. Their isolation turned into a dedication to convert the tribes. Sometimes, we whispered, it was the missionaries who needed to be saved. We lived in a world of comedies, thunderstorms, chances like a flight of passenger pigeons over the lake, and surprises, dreams about whales in a fish barrel. Some of our friends think it is strange to find pale, weak and shadowless, individual church heroes, in the middle of old woodland families. The biblical stories were fun to tell, the old men turned them over in the oral tradition. The moral lessons that end in words end in comedies. These missionaries were never loons, never bears, their wives and mothers were never killdeers on the shoreline. We were animals and birds, even when we were converted, and that was the difference between culture and civilization. We once spoke the language of animals, the missionaries were caught in word-winds.

Reverend Hall, of course, was proud of his religion but he was disappointed with the tribes. We could all tell when he was displeased with us because two small muscles would twitch on his face. He liked us, he spoke our names from time to time when he visited the schoolroom, and he even called us scholars in his reports. He said our names were in his reports and that we would be known in the government. We knew he cared more for us and other mixedblood families at La Pointe than he did for the tribal families on Chequamegon Point and the Bad River Reservation. He reported to a government agent that the mission school there was "discontinued for want of scholars. . . . We regret to see so little interest taken by these Indians in the subject of education. Most of them attach little or no importance to having their children instructed. I have been informed that many of the head men have expressed a desire to have their school money divided among them, as their other annuities are, that they might expend it in the same way. . . .

"In some respects these Indians are improving. Many of them are adopting partial habits of civilization. This is more and more apparent every year in their mode of dress, in their efforts to procure houses to live in, and in their enlarging their gardens and small fields. Many are much more industrious than formerly, and are much less disposed to depend on the same precarious modes of obtaining the means of subsistence, which almost universally prevailed among them formerly. These changes are most apparent among the younger portion of them.

"If the right kind of influences are brought to bear upon them, and they can be shielded from the degrading and destroying evils of intoxicating drink, I do not see why they may not eventually become a civilized and happy people. This however must be the work of time, and will require much perseverance on the part of those who are disposed to live among them for the purpose of teaching them letters, the arts, and the Christian religion."

M A R G A R E T   C A
A N G E L I C K   F R O

The narrow waves from the wake of the steamer washed over the last few letters of our names printed in the sand. We collect names and words, some are secrets, but we take much more time to remember the clothes that visitors wear, their hats and shoes and coats. The trunks on the dock, unloaded from the steamer, capture our attention for hours. We imagine the contents of the arriving trunks, and we dream we are on an adventure to the cities inside the departing trunks.

When Reverend Hall and his wife first arrived, the content of their trunks and boxes became the talk of the island, but the secrets lasted for a few minutes at the most because they owned little more than their simple clothes. The Warren families gave them some furniture, a washbowl and stand, chairs, tables, and a bedstead, for their little house. "It is not the deprivation of the conveniences of life," he wrote to his friends back east, "that makes us feel more sensibly that we are in a heathen land. It is the want of society. There are not more than three or four, besides our own family, with whom we can communicate in our native tongue at this place."

Madeline Island is our tribal home, the place where the earth began, the place that first came back from the flood. Naanabozho, the trickster, was born here, on this island; the old men told us he was the first little person in the world. He stole fire from across the lake. We are little people. This is our place on the earth, this place is in our bodies, in our words, and in our dreams. Our new names, there in the sand, hold back the next flood, but nothing holds back the tall people who come from the East. Naanabozho must have stolen fire from them; now the tall white people are here and they want the whole earth back as punishment.

Even so, we love to watch white visitors and the dark trunks that come on the steamer from the East, and to listen to the stories at the American Fur Company store across from the dock.

Abba Spooner will think we are late because we were making maple sugar, or something, or we could tell her that we were with the priest for religious instruction.

The Catholic church is located behind the American Fur Company store and warehouses. A high stockade fence surrounds a fruit and vegetable garden and separates the sacred from the secular commercial world of the tall people. The priest lives near the church in a small house built of hewn logs because frame houses are much too expensive to build on the island. The cemetery is next to the church.

A visitor to the island told about how the little people buried the dead in grave houses. "On the whole, it can be truly said that they have more regard for the dead than many whites have. The pagans used to bury various articles used by the deceased during life, also place tobacco or sugar on the grave, or in the drawer made for that purpose in the little house built over the grave. But these customs are falling into disuse more and more. A peculiar feeling or sadness and pity seizes one in passing a pagan grave-yard. . . ."

White children, sons of the missionaries, would raid the grave houses at night and steal the food, a confection with cooked wild rice and maple sugar, the little people placed there.

Right Reverend Frederic Baraga, an Austrian sent by the Leopoldine Society in Vienna, was not welcomed by the lonesome ministers on the island. The first mission resisted encroachment and hoped that Henry Rowe Schoolcraft, the government agent, would refuse the priest a "license of residence." Schoolcraft did not respond; the priest moved to the island and built a church in less than two weeks. During the summer, as if his time there was limited, Father Baraga had baptized more than a hundred mixedbloods and tribal people.

Reverend Sherman Hall wrote to the secretary of the American Board of Commissioners for Foreign Missions in Boston – the little people were considered foreign – that "the Catholics were not prejudiced against the mission school. The priest stationed here encourages their attendance."

Father Francis Pierz, who had established missions at several fur trade posts in the woodland, visited the island that summer. He admired the garden behind the fur post and, of course, the new church and mission. His neck and back caused him pain as he walked. No one seemed to notice, so eager were they to present their accomplishments in the wilderness. He blessed the children when he passed them and complimented those who worked on the island. Later, in a letter he described his experiences with more candor. "A large trading company has a branch store on this island and it is therefore the rendezvous of many Indians and French-Canadians, all of whom lived like pagans before Father Baraga's arrival.

"At first this pious missionary had to contend with many difficulties and hardships, but with his customary, persevering energy and apostolic zeal he soon formed out of these rude, wild barbarians a very large Christian congregation, which continues to grow daily through new conversions. To his great joy he has completed his beautiful new church and a suitable priest's house with the money he brought with him from Europe. . . .

"As regards my own personal experience, having had many opportunities during my three years' stay among the Indians of several places to watch them, pagans as well as Christians, I can justly assert that they are, as a rule, phlegmatic, good-natured, exceedingly patient and docile, and well disposed to lead a good life. Even in their wild, aboriginal state, when they are removed from bad, scandalous people, they do not live at all wickedly and viciously. They listen eagerly to the priest who comes to them, readily embrace the faith, and allow themselves to be soon transformed into good, steadfast Christians.

"But where the poor Indians have been scandalized by the great vices of white Christians, or have been spoiled by intoxicating liquor, and have been seduced by the enemies of religion and prejudiced against our holy faith, they naturally become far harder to convert and civilize. . . ."

Father Baraga was a little man with enormous conversion plans for the tribe. His dark brown hair bounced in long curls as he walked. He was firm, careful in his speech, and when he was out walking on the road, his short legs moved quicker than a shore bird. He was determined to save souls and he warned the teachers at the mission school that "if they meddle with religion I would order all the Catholic children to leave their schools; and I am watching strictly this observance."

The little priest was troubled by tribal manners and woodland culture. He abhorred the wilderness in their lives, and describes cruelties that he relates to savagism. He praised the little people who followed the cross and disapproved of those tribal people who gathered on the island for government payments. The priest even cursed the tribal dances that healed the soul, restored tribal shadows near tall people, and earned a meal. The missionaries rebuked the presentation of bare flesh, rhythmic body movements, and imaginative face paint. Church strictures soon became government policies. The tribes were not permitted to gather to dance.

Julia Spears, the daughter of Lyman Marcus Warren, would have none of this bad talk from the missionaries about tribal dances. She remembers a more peaceful island than did the missionaries. Julia was also known by her tribal nickname Conians, which means "little money" in translation.

Several thousand tribal people came to Madeline Island from various places around the lake to receive government payments according to agreements in treaties. "That year the Indians received ten dollars a head," Julia Spears wrote, "and each family got a very large bundle of goods. . . . They had rations issued out to them during payment. . . . The day before they would start for their homes they had a custom of going to all the stores and houses and dancing for about one hour, expecting food to be given to them. . . . They went around in different parties of about twenty-five or thirty. A party came to our house at the old fort. We were prepared for them. The day before, we cooked a lot of bread, a lot of boiled salt pork and cookies to give them. They came dancing and hooting. They were naked with breechclothes, their bodies painted with black, red, yellow, vermillion, with all kinds of stripes and figures.

"They were a fierce looking crowd. They were all good dancers. After they were through they sat down on the grass and smoked. We gave them their *wapoo* and they were well pleased. They thanked us and shook hands with us as they left." The word *wapoo*, or *wabo*, from the oral tradition, at the end of some words in *anashinaabemowin* denotes fluid or liquid, as in the word *mashkikiwabo*, a liquid medicine, or *ishkotewabo*, "firewater," or an alcoholic drink, according to *A Dictionary of the Otchipwe Language* by Right Reverend Bishop Baraga who was a missionary on the island at this time more than a century ago. Nichols and Nyholm transcribe the word for liquor as *ishkodewaaboo* in *Ojibwewi-Ikidowinan*.

We waited on the dock near the steamboat until no one was watching and then we climbed into two huge brown trunks with bright brass corners. The sun leaped through thin cracks and seams on the curved truck cover, enough light inside to read our secret maps, the ones we charted with places from all the stories we had heard in the store: all the mixed-blood routes and portage places between land and lakes and fur posts.

We were silent, alone, breathless, counting our rapid heart beats past the island view, past the distant shores of the lake and over the picture mountains to the cities in the East. We smelled smoke and imagined a circus show with actors and clowns, but instead it was the trader and his dock hands, the ones with the little pighead pipes, smoking their strong tobacco.

We traveled to Fond du Lac.

We listened.

Shingabaossin, an orator of the Crane family from Sault St. Marie, was the first to speak to the tribal leaders and to the tall white men, Lewis

Cass and Thomas McKenney, who were treaty commissioners; and Henry Rowe Schoolcraft, the government agent, and others at Fond du Lac where hundreds of tribal people came together late in the summer to talk about mixedbloods and minerals.

The tribal orator told about other meetings, and agreed that land should be provided for mixedbloods, and then his voice seemed to disappear on the wind when he said that, "our fathers have come here to embrace their children. Listen to what they say. It will be good for you.

"If you have any copper on your lands," said Shingabaossin in a distant voice as he looked over the commissioners to the western horizon where thunderclouds were blooming, "I advise you to sell it. It is of no advantage to us. They can convert it into articles for our use. If any one of you has any knowledge on this subject, I ask you to bring it to light. . . ."

William Whipple Warren, the mixedblood historian, wrote that Shingabaossin did not mean what was attributed to him in translation. When the orator referred to minerals it was "meant more to tickle the ears of the commissioners and to obtain their favor, than as an earnest appeal to his people, for the old chieftain was too much imbued with the superstition prevalent amongst the Indians, which prevents them from discovering their knowledge of minerals and copper boulders to the whites."

Tribal leaders, nevertheless, signed a treaty there that provided in part that the "Chippewa tribe grant to the government of the United States the right to search for, and carry away, any metals or minerals from any part of their country. . . ." The leaders must have believed in the spiritual power of secrets, the unspoken in the oral tradition, because what is held in secrets cannot be discovered and removed. Copper was located in sacred places, the metal had not been used in the secular production of material possessions. The elders signed an agreement on paper, through a translator, but did not tell the white men where the copper could be found.

Pezeekee spoke that morning to the white men who sat behind tables, dressed in dark clothes. The elder from La Pointe placed his right hand over his left forearm and looked toward Henry Connor, the government interpreter, and watched him write down in translation the words he heard. Pezeekee remembered the wind in the bullrushes and turned his words with care. "The name of a speaker has come down to me from my fathers," he said to the commissioners.

"I will not lie.

"That sun that looks upon me, and these, you red children around

me, are witnesses. . . . Our women and children are very poor. You have
heard it. It need not have been said. You see it. . . . I lend those who
have put me here, my mouth. . . .

"This was given to us by our forefathers," he said as he spread a map
on the table before the commissioners and interpreters. "There are few
now here who were then living." He directed the tall men at the table
to notice certain places on the map, tribal communities, memories in
space. Then he looked up from the map and over the heads of the tall
men. He spoke to them but did not look into their faces. Small clouds
seemed to speak through the white pine on the horizon. "You have
deserted *your* country," he told the commissioners, looking past their
faces. "Where your fathers lived, and your mothers first saw the sun,
there you are not. I am alone, am the solitary one remaining on our own
ground. . . .

"I am no chief," Pezeekee said and then paused to listen. "I am put
here as a speaker. The gift has descended to me. . . . It will be long before
I open my mouth to you again. Listen, therefore, to what I say. I live
in one place, I do not move about. I live on an open path, where many
walk. The traders know me. None can say I ever looked in his cabin or
his canoe. My hands are free from the touch of what does not belong
to me. . . ."

Pezeekee recovered his map and there was silence.

Then an old man who did not reveal his tribal name told the commissioners that he did not sell the sacred earth for a peace medal and
a flag from the government agents. He was troubled, his voice wavered
as he spoke: "You told me to sit still and hold down my head, and if I
heard bad birds singing, to bend it still lower.

"My friends held down their heads when I approached. When I
turned, bad words went out of their mouths against me. I could not sit
still. I left the cabin, and went out alone into the wild woods," the old
man said as he looked down from time to time at the weeds. "There have
I remained, till I heard of your coming. I am here now, to take you by
the hand. . . ."

The commissioners were silent.

Obarguwack moved toward the commissioners at the table. She was
in her seventies. Her bones were old, and it took her twice the time to
walk and talk than it did when she was younger. She said that she was
blessed with her age, to live so long was not a curse, she reminded the
commissioners as they watched her slow movements. The wrinkles on
her face all seemed to converge at her mouth, and when she spoke, and
paused to compose her thoughts, the wrinkles moved from her mouth
like ripples expanding from the place a stone skipped on calm water. She

told the commissioners seated at the table under the trees that she was representing her husband. "His eyes are shut, but his mouth and ears are still open," she said and then paused a second time to move a few more steps closer to the table. "He has long wished to see the Americans. He hopes now to find something in his cabin.

"He has held you by the hand," she told the tall white men. "He still holds you by the hand. He is poor. His blanket is old and worn out, like the one you see." She paused again and moved a few steps closer to the commissioners behind the table to show them the worn blanket she mentioned. "But he now thinks he sees a better one."

The commissioners waited in silence for a few minutes until the old woman moved back from the table and then the meeting was adjourned until the next day when a treaty would be prepared for signatures. The commissioners listened, but what the government wanted had been decided in advance. The experiences of tribal people were translated from the oral tradition, but there was little more than condescension in the manners of the commissioners. The simple needs of the tribes, blankets, a place of peace on the earth, medical assistance, were no match under the trees in the word wars to locate and possess minerals and natural resources.

James Otis Lewis drew pictures of the tribal people who spoke and while the treaty was being read in translation by a government interpreter. The flags in his pictures were all taller than the trees behind the table. Colonel Thomas McKenney bumped his knee on the corner of the table as he sat down, prepared to make histories on paper. He looked toward the eastern horizon, in the opposite direction of the tribal people there, with a mark of pain on his face while he listened and waited. Then he looked toward the artist, finding more to consider in a face on paper than in tribal events in the oral tradition. He brushed his thick hair back from his forehead, white strands in the red. Even his hand in his own hair seemed unnatural that afternoon at Fond du Lac.

We remember article four of the treaty:

It being deemed important that the half-breeds, scattered through this extensive country, should be stimulated to exertion and improvement by the possession of permanent property and fixed residences, the Chippewa tribe, in consideration of the affection they bear to these persons, and of the interest which they feel in their welfare, grant to each of the persons described . . . six hundred and forty acres of land. . . .

"The objects of the commissioners were easily attained," wrote William Whipple Warren in his book *History of the Ojibway Nation*, "but the Ojibways, who felt a deep love for the offspring of their women who had intermarried with the whites, and cherished them as their own children, insisted on giving them grants of land on the Sault St. Marie River, which they wished our government to recognize and make good.

"These stipulations were annexed by the commissioners to the treaty, but were never ratified by the Senate of the United States. It is merely mentioned here to show the great affection with which the Ojibways regarded their half-breeds, and which they have evinced on every occasion when they have had an opportunity of bettering their condition."

Eighty-five tribal leaders from fifteen different woodland communities signed their marks beneath the signatures of Lewis Cass and Thomas McKenney to a treaty at Fond du Lac in the presence of fourteen white men, two of whom were official commissioners. The tribal leaders, who were awarded peace medals to remember the occasion, were from La Pointe, Rainy Lake, Lac du Flambeau, Ontonagon, Vermilion Lake, River de Corbeau, and other places. The white men were from the East. John Quincy Adams, then president of the United States, signed the treaty, with the exception of the articles that provided for mixedblood people.

We imagined our names on these treaties, we marked these places on our personal dream maps, places the old mixedbloods told about in their stories around the stove at the store. . . . *To each of the children of John Tanner, being of Chippewa descent. . . . To Charlotte Louisa Morrison, wife of Allan Morrison. . . . To Saugemauqua, widow of the late John Baptiste Cadotte, and to her children Louison, Sophia, Archangel, Edward, and Polly, one section each . . . upon the islands and shore of the Saint Mary river wherever good land enough for this purpose can be found. . . .* Our places on the dream maps, our shadows in the stories.

Slivers of sunlight shivered inside the trunks as we were loaded from the dock to the steamboat. Dock men commented on the weight of the possessions of the tall people from the East. Inside the trunks we listened to conversations on the dock and on the deck of the steamboat as people boarded. Comments on the weather, how severe had been the last winter, arrival times at the next ports and fur posts on the lake. We listened and counted our heartbeats, faster and faster across the lake and over the mountains, in a horse-drawn carriage, alone in the parlour of a tall frame house, a mansion with double lace curtains and with windows in the doors. In each trunk we found a parasol, high button boots, fine clothes, hat boxes, and a small chest with precious stones. We imagined the world at the end of the lake where the steamboat stopped for the last time.

The steamboat whistle sounded several times, breathless at the dock, the last invitation to those still on the shore. The sound of the steam whistle was muffled inside the trunks, and each sound was a new port, a new dock, new faces, places on our dream maps. We walked down each dock beneath new parasols, our shadows traveled across the earth.

The steamboat moved from the dock. We could hear conversations on the side of the deck and we could imagine from the dark interior of the trunks all the people on the dock. Our friends from school were there, the old mixedbloods who would tell stories about us in the store, the little priest, all waving to us as we leave the island for the first time. Our names held back the flood at the first place we knew on the earth. We will be remembered forever.

THREE ANISHINAABEG WRITERS

■

The craving for historical identity is not in any sense a people's movement. . . . Ethnic writers have concentrated on an abstract craving for historical identity. . . . I am afraid, therefore, one must characterize this ethnic movement as upperclass intellectual romanticism. Like all romanticism, it serves conservative and, in fact, reactionary interests.

Gunnar Myrdal,
The Center Magazine

■

WILLIAM WHIPPLE WARREN

■

William Whipple Warren, mixedblood interpreter, historian, legislator, was seventeen years of age when he first observed a sacred tribal relic, a circular copper plate exhibited by the elder Tugwaugaunay at La Pointe on Madeline Island. There were eight marks, or indentations, on the copper plate, Warren remembers, each mark denoting one generation since the Anishinaabeg first lived on the island.

"By the rude figure of a man with a hat on its head, placed opposite one of these indentations, was denoted the period when the white race first made his appearance among them," Warren wrote in his *History of the Ojibway Nation*. "This mark occurred in the third generation, leaving five generations which had passed away since that important era in their history."

Warren, who was the son of Lyman Marcus Warren, attended the mission school at La Pointe on Madeline Island where he learned to speak the language of the Anishinaabeg. His brother Truman was also an interpreter. His sister Mary was a teacher at the Red Lake Reservation, and his sister Julia, who wrote about her memories of the tribal dances on the island, taught school on the White Earth Reservation.

Mary, his mother, wife of Lyman Marcus Warren and the daughter of Michel Cadotte, invited her maternal uncle Tugwaugaunay to show the copper plate, which had been buried in a secret tribal place. When Warren, and his mother and father, saw the copper plate, the tribal elder returned it to the earth, a sacred place. No one has seen the plate since then.

Tugwaugaunay was about sixty years of age at the time he presented the copper plate, which he said had descended to him "direct through a long line of ancestors." Tugwaugaunay "died two years since, and his death had added the ninth indentation . . . nine generations since the Ojibway first resided at La Pointe, and six generations since their first intercourse with the whites. . . .

"The Ojibways never count a generation as passed away till the oldest man in the family has died, and the writer assumes from these, and other facts obtained through observation and inquiry, forty years as the term of an Indian generation. It is necessary to state, however, for the benefit of those who may consider this an over-estimate, that, since the introduction of intoxicating drinks and diseases of the whites, the former well-authenticated longevity of the Indians has been materially lessened.

"According to this estimate, it is now three hundred and sixty years since the Ojibways first collected in one grand central town on the island of La Pointe, and two hundred and forty years since they were first discovered by the white race," Warren wrote in his history, which was first published a century ago by the Minnesota Historical Society.

William Warren was born at La Pointe on May 27, 1825, and died twenty-eight years later at the home of his sister in Saint Paul. At the age of eighteen he married Matilda Aitkin, who was the daughter of the trader William Aitkin. Two years later he moved with his family to Minnesota. The family lived first at Crow Wing, then at Gull Lake, before establishing their home at Two Rivers. He was employed as a farmer and interpreter. In January 1851 he appeared at the state legislature in Saint Paul to take "his seat as a member of the House of Representatives," according to a memoir written by J. Fletcher Williams. "Up to this time he had been quite unknown to the public men and pioneers of the Territory, but by his engaging manners, and frank, candid disposition, soon won a large circle of friends. . . . Had his life and health been spared," Williams continues, Warren "would have made important contributions to the knowledge which we possess regarding the history, customs, and religion of the aboriginal inhabitants of Minnesota. He had projected at least two other works . . . and it is believed that he had the material, and the familiarity with the subject, to have completed them in a thorough manner."

Tugwaugaunay, the elder who presented the virgin copper plate, was the head chief of the Crane family, "a very modest and retiring man," according to Warren, who, with his mother and father, saw the plate for the last time. "I am the only one still alive who witnessed," he wrote more than a century ago, "this sacred relic of former days."

The plate was made from copper mined near the island. The tribes did not mine the mineral as a source of private wealth; the copper was used in sacred rites and ceremonies. White men made it their official business to locate minerals, but tribal people were secretive about the places copper could be found. Centuries before white people arrived on the island, the tribes mined copper. Some of the mines and open sites were identified on tribal maps, and others were told and remembered in the oral tradition, but most of the sites were sacred places on the earth. At some of these places, huge chunks of copper were exposed. There were several copper sites on the Ontonagon River, but not all of them were sacred. For example, the location of a five hundred ton nugget of copper in the river was no secret, but other sites on the river were sacred, where shamans and healers came to dream and seek their visions. Anishinaabeg elders came to the sacred copper sites in the late spring to heal their bones. Copper held healing spirits, the best energies of the earth. Some healers prescribed the cold river water than ran through the exposed copper stone as a source of health and mythic dreams.

The tall men, however, the explorers from the East, had different ideas about the values of copper. A small mine could make a man rich in the world. A white man could live in comfort in the East with a mine in the West.

"Now, about that copper rock in the Ontonagon River," said Antoine Perrinier to Father Baraga at La Pointe. James Jamison wrote about the priest and mentioned the curiosities over copper in his book, *By Cross and Anchor: The Story of Frederic Baraga on Lake Superior*.

"I have never seen it, but it is there," Bishop Baraga responded. "Yes, it is solid copper. Several Indians who have seen it have told me about it."

The Anishinaabeg "do not like to talk about that copper rock," said Charles Oakes, aware that some of the copper sites were sacred to the tribe. "I myself have never seen it. It is quite a distance up the river, I am told. Oh yes, I am certain that such a copper rock exists. For my part, I say let it stay there."

Government agents, however, did not share the view of Charles Oakes, who was the fur trader from La Pointe. Even the first white explorers noted the value of copper in the woodland lakes. Not all white men were deceptive and avaricious, but even with a positive historical view of civilized movements from the East, the woodland tribes in the middle of the nineteenth century were separated from their sacred places on the earth. White people were determined to exploit animals, human beings, minerals, the sacred, in their pursuit of wealth and domination, their manifest destinies perceived in the woodland.

Commissioners Lewis Cass and Thomas Loraine McKenney, and Henry Rowe Schoolcraft, United States Indian Agent, concluded a treaty at Fond du Lac, then in Michigan Territory, which states in the third article that "The Chippewa tribe grant to the government of the United States the right to search for, and carry away, any metals or minerals from any part of their country. But this grant is not to affect the title of the land, nor the existing jurisdiction over it."

George Porter departed for the Ontonagon River, *four days before the treaty was signed*, "for the purpose of procuring the mass of native copper," he wrote in a letter to the treaty commissioner. "This remarkable specimen of virgin copper lies a little above low water mark on the west bank of the river and about thirty-five miles from its mouth. Its appearance is brilliant wherever the metal is visible. It consists of pure copper, ramified in every direction through a mass of stone . . . in veins of from one to three inches in diameter; and, in some parts, exhibiting masses of pure metal of one hundred pounds weight, but so intimately connected with the surrounding body, that it was found impossible to detach them with any instruments which we had provided. . . ."

Porter and his detachment found the first copper stone in the river, the same stone that others had attempted to locate in the past. This copper stone, at an obvious place in the river, was presented to white men in tribal stories, even presented in tribal maps as a distraction so that white men would not seek the sacred copper sites on other parts of the river.

Douglass Houghton, a geologist and explorer, reported five years later in a letter to Lewis Cass that he had found a "mass of copper," which lies "partly covered by water, directly at the foot of a clay hill, from which, together with numerous boulders of the primitive rocks, it has undoubtedly been washed by the action of the water of the river. . . .

"Several smaller masses of insulated native copper have been discovered on the borders of Lake Superior, but that upon Ontonagon River is the only one which is now known to remain."

KAHGEGAGAHBOWH: GEORGE COPWAY

■

"An Indian author!" exclaimed a writer in his notice about *The Life, History, and Travels of Kah-ge-ga-gah-bowh*, published more than a century ago by

James Harmstead in Philadelphia. "If he should immortalize himself by his writings, the literary world will be puzzled to pronounce his name.

"Kah-ge-ga-gah-bowh!

"What a jaw breaker!

"It is worse than Spanish. Yet the bearer of this euphonious name has written a very creditable book, and a very interesting one too, and a very handsome one into the bargain. There are some passages of decided beauty in it, that remind us of specimens that have frequently been published of Indian eloquence. . . ."

Kahgegagahbowh, also known as George Copway, told white people more than they wanted to hear or know about tribal people then, but they listened in the good graces of their missions and elite stations and read his books because he seemed to be an exception to his race. The white world embraced him with romantic and political care; understood him, in simple racial terms, not because he had renounced his tribal origins as a savage, which he had not, but because he was one of the first ordained tribal missionaries to work in the woodland communities he once claimed to be his tribal home.

Copway was a handsome man with a clear and articulate voice, and he was a skilled writer. In his lectures and publications, which reached an international audience, he demonstrated how well he had listened to the lessons of those white missionaries and woodland evangelists he first met when he was a child. His teachers then brought to him an ecstatic new world view with original sin and salvation of the soul. The subtitle of his first book, *A Young Indian Chief of the Ojebwa Nation, A Convert to the Christian Faith, and a Missionary to his People for Twelve Years; with a Sketch of the Present State of the Ojebwa Nation, in Regard to Christianity and their Future Prospects* is no less a testament to his new religious experiences, spiritual fervor, and conversion schemes in the woodland. "*Also, an Appeal; with all the Names of the Chiefs Now Living, who have been Christianized, and the Missionaries now Laboring among them*," appears on the title page of the second edition of his first book.

Copway reveals in his book that his conversion took place when he was twelve years old, in the summer following the death of his mother. She had been bedridden with consumption for several months, and then, "just before her death she prayed with her children, and advised us to be good Christians, to love Jesus, and meet her in heaven. She then sang her favorite hymn.

Jesus ish pe ming kah e zhod.

Jesus, my all, to heaven is gone.

"This was the first hymn she heard or learned; and it is on this account that I introduce and sing this sweet hymn whenever I lecture on the origin, history, traditions, migration, and customs, of the Ojebwa nation. . . ."

Copway remembered that sublime moment of his own conversion which took place at a religious camp where he had gone with his father. There was a thunderstorm, he mentioned lightning and rain, and wrote that "my father held me by the hand. . . . We had to walk thirty miles . . . in order to reach the place of destination.

"Multitudes of Indians, and a large concourse of whites from various places, were on the ground when we arrived. In the evening, one of the white preachers spoke . . . of the plain and good road to heaven; of the characters that were walking in it; he then spoke of the bad place. . . .

"I now began to feel as if I should die; *I felt very sick in my heart* . . . I was deeply distressed, and knew not the cause," he wrote. Then he knelt at the roots of a tree while his father prayed for him. The storm ended, and the frightened child recollected that he felt like a *"wounded bird*, fluttering for its life. . . .

"The small brilliant light came near to me, and fell upon my head, and then ran all over and through me, just as if water had been copiously poured out upon me . . . my head was in a puddle of water, in a small ditch. . . .

"I clapped my hands, and exclaimed in English, *Glory to Jesus.*" Copway wrote about the instant of his conversion. "I looked around for my father, and saw him. I told him that I had found Jesus. He embraced me and kissed me. . . . I felt as strong as a lion, yet as humble as a poor Indian boy saved by grace, by grace alone. . . ."

Following his conversion in the woods, he studied with his father, attended numerous evangelical meetings, and in time he traveled to the east for further instruction and direction. He studied with white religious leaders, and returned to the woodland, the tribal communities he knew as a child, with a new mission. He was now a religious reformer with the single ambition to convert the tribes.

The memories and personal experiences he reveals in his letters, lectures, and books, are romantic, idealized, closer to the benevolent descriptions of the tribes offered by white writers, then and now, rather than a landscape of mythic tribal events or a frame for the ironies and contradictions of human survival under the cultural duress of missionaries and colonial apologists. Copway was a keen survivor, material and spiritual, but tribal missionaries who base their ken on conversion, as he did, cast strange shadows on familiar woodland trails.

In a foreword to the reader, Copway wrote that he was "a stranger in a strange land! And often, when the sun is sinking in the western sky, I think of my former home; my heart yearns for the loved of other days, and tears flow like the summer rain. How the heart of the wanderer and pilgrim, after long years of absence, beats, and his eyes fill, as he catches a glance at the hills of his nativity, and reflects upon the time when he pressed the lips of a mother, or sister, now cold in death. . . .

Copway was separated from his tribal origins. He seemed driven by his sense of strangeness; his success in the dominant cultures of the world was not without some sorrow and an impression of loss. He was a persuasive speaker, moved by his differences in public; he was motivated by his twists and sudden bends of personal experience where others might have expired or turned meek. Finding an audience pleased him; he demonstrated his personal power to others, convincing himself in time. When he tired of simple woodland listeners in tribal communities, he turned to politics and practiced his handsome metaphors on broader solutions to the problems of the tribes. He traveled and lectured, and the more he was praised in the cities, the less he celebrated thunderstorms and the moments of his simple conversion in the woodland.

"During my residence of six years among the pale faces," he writes in the introduction to *The Traditional History and Characteristic Sketches of the Ojibway Nation*, published in London by Charles Gilpin, "I have acquired a knowledge of men and things, much, very much more I have yet to learn, and it is my desire that my brethren in the far west may share with me my crust of information; for this end I have laboured and do labour, and will continue to labour, till success crowns my efforts or my voice and hand are silent in the home of the departed. . . .

"Education and Christianity are to the Indian what wings are to the eagle; they elevate him; and these given to him by men of right views of existence enable him to rise above the soil of degradation, and hover about the high mounts of wisdom and truth. . . ."

Copway was born in the fall of 1818 near the Trent River in Canada where his parents were "attending the annual distribution of the presents from the government to the Indians.

"My parents were of the Ojebwa nation, who lived on the lake back of Cobourg, on the shores of Lake Ontario, Canada West. . . . My father and mother were taught the religion of their nation. My father became a medicine man in the early part of his life, and always had by him the implements of war, which generally distinguished our head men. He was as good a hunter as any in the tribe. . . .

"My great grandfather was the first who ventured to settle at Rice Lake, after the Ojebwa nation defeated the Hurons, who once inhabited all the lakes in Western Canada, and who had a large village just on the top of the hill . . . a magnificent view of the lakes and surrounding country. He was of the Crane tribe . . . had a crane for totem . . . which now forms the totem of the villagers, excepting those who have since come amongst us from other villages by intermarriage, for there was a law that no one was to marry one of the same totem. . . .

"My grandfather lived here about this time, and held some friendly intercourse with the whites. My father here learned the manners, customs, and worship of the nation. He, and others, became acquainted with the early settlers, and have ever been friendly with the whites. And I know the day when he used to shake the hand of the white man, and, *very friendly*, the white man would say, *take some whiskey*. . . .

"My mother was of the Eagle tribe; she was a sensible woman; she was as good a hunter as any of the Indians; she could shoot the deer, and the ducks flying, as well as they. Nature had done a great deal for her, for she was active; and she was much more cleanly than the majority of our women in those days. She lived to see the day when most of her children were given up to the Lord in Christian baptism; while she experienced a change of heart, and the fulness of God in man, for she lived daily in the enjoyment of God's favors. . . .

I was born in nature's wide domain! The trees were all that sheltered my infant limbs—the blue heavens all that covered me. I am one of Nature's children; I have always admired her; she shall be my glory; her features . . . all contribute to my enduring love of her; and wherever I see her, emotions of pleasure roll in my breast, and swell and burst like waves on the shores of the ocean, in prayer and praise to Him who has placed me in her hand. . . ."

In the end, there were no roads back home to the place of his insecure tribal birth. At the moment of his conversion in a thunderstorm he lost the familiar angles of shared metaphors, the natural seams and wind checks in a woodland tribal world view that can sustain the most radical and troubled wanderers. Copway was imaginative, serious in his missions, an admired man at last, and dedicated to finding the meaning of his past in abstract generalizations, to discovering and explaining his experiences in political proposals. Thin clouds on the horizon, even thunderstorms, pass for memories, but since his conversion he was like a bird that had migrated too soon on a cold wind, or he was like the leaves on a small tree that turned with the first frost; the world could see what he had done with his soul and shadow in the woodland. There was little time to turn back; he could only remember in printed words at a great distance from the oral tradition. Those who remained at the treeline noticed his transformation from totem to titles since his conversion. At the end of all his speeches, letters, and political ideas, his books, he must have been alone, separated in the dualities and cruelties of a new place.

Copway is remembered in words, in the historical power of a written language. He changed the metaphors from his past, but not mythic tribal time.

In his speeches and in four editorial letters he proposes a resolution to the problems of tribal people. In linear topical form, his four letters focus on why tribal people have not improved with exposure to white culture; the possession of land in the west; a proposal for a new tribal nation; and the benefits, as he saw them, to tribal people, settlers, and the government. He was ahead of his time in understanding land problems and cultural conflicts, but he had no political constituencies to embrace his ideas. His mission was applauded but not enacted.

Copway points out in his first letter that "teaching the Indians in their own language what little some have learned, is one of those errors in which the majority of missionaries have fallen. . . . I have endeavored to persuade them to teach our people English. . . . A great amount of time, and a tremendous amount of money has been expended in translating and publishing a few books. . . .

"I conclude this part of my letter by stating that the most requisite things for the Indians are these three: a mechanical or an agricultural education, a high-toned literature, and a rational moral training. Give him these—you make him exalted. Deprive him of these—you make him degraded."

The missionaries, he argues, should better understand tribal experiences, and explains that the "Indian not knowing abstract truths, cannot possibly understand the foundation of the many doctrinal views which he is desired to learn and adopt. . . . Take him as he is, and lead him, and he will soon see the right from the wrong. We want also educated men. It has been the idea of some that any thing will do for the Indians."

In his second editorial letter he shows concern that tribal lands could be claimed again and again by settlers in the west. "Where will the Indian go to get any thing to feed his children. . . . The game is being killed more and more every year. . . .

"Where there is no stimulus to improve, there will be no idea of learning much. In small bodies, they retain all the feelings of their forefathers, and will continue this way. The American government has addressed us like different nations, and as one family; they have in this way perpetuated our differences towards each other. . . .

Copway asserts, in his third letter to the editor, that his "objective is to induce the general government to locate the Indians in a collective body, where, after they are secured in their lands, they may make such improvements as shall serve to attach them to their homes. . . .

"The location which I have chosen for their home, is the unsettled land, known as the north-west territory, between the territories of

Nebraska and Minnesota, on the eastern banks of the Missouri River. . . ."
He points out that tribal people are a "social race. They would rather live
in large bodies than in small ones, particularly when they are partially
civilized. The oftener they see one another, the more rapidly would their
jealousies cease to exist. . . ." The woodland tribes he believes would be
adapted to such a state because of their language similarities. "This is
one of the best appeals I made to them when I visited them. Tradition
says we were all one people once, and now to be reunited will be a great
social blessing. Wars must then cease."

Copway invited a proclamation from the President of the United
States to all the woodland tribes "to till the ground as they must soon
have recourse to farming for a living, would induce them individually
to go without the chiefs, and they would, as soon as they entered the
new territory, frame laws founded on republicanism. . . ."

In conclusion, he outlines the values and advantages of his proposal
for a collective tribal nation. The government would save money, he emphasizes; the administration of tribal business would be simplified; the
government would not have to maintain forts at scattered tribal communities; and "besides the above considerations, there are higher motives
which ought to prompt the members of Congress—motives arising in the
consideration that they are only forwarding the great design of Heaven,
to improve the races of this country.

"By intelligence enlarge the arena of human freedom," he concludes,
with no obvious ironies, "and your leading the Indian will be like the
noble eagle's first flight with its young to the sun." Such hyperbole must
have calmed the most insecure and outrageous discussions.

The advantages to the tribes are presented in romantic advertisements, the broadsides of colonial apologists. "By having *permanent*
homes, they would soon enjoy the fruit of their labour. Poverty would
be unknown, plenty would reign, and cheerfulness aid them in their
work. . . . The result of all this would be a rapid increase of intelligence
among the Indians, and steps would soon be taken to have a representa-
tion in Congress."

Copway advanced these ideas in various places, here and in other
nations. In England, for example, the *Liverpool Standard* on July 30, 1850,
devoted several columns to his speech at the Brunswick Chapel. The
following week he spoke in the lecture hall at the Mechanics' Institution.
"An Indian chief of the Ojibway nation," the *Liverpool Mercury* reported,
"made a very interesting and powerful appeal to the numerous audience
on behalf of his plan for concentrating, civilizing, and Christianizing the
Indians of the north-west territory of America, on land to be set apart
to their use in perpetuity by the government of the United States. . . .

He also related some very affecting anecdotes, consequent on the cruel conduct pursued by the whites in forcing the removal of the Indians from their own territory to the westward. . . . Copway then alluded to the coercive measures adopted to drive the Indians from their homes, adding that the so-called legal acts of the white men would shame the devil himself; for he considered him more of a gentleman than to be guilty of such acts.

"In the second place, the feeling of the white people towards the Indian was getting better," the *Liverpool Mercury* story continues, "and although there had been such an eternal hatred against the Indian, many of the white men were as bad, and could sound the war-whoop as well as the coloured men. When the white people saw that they could make nothing of the Indians by harsh means, and tried rationally to educate them, and teach them agriculture, they listened patiently. . . .

"In consequence of a letter which he had written, he saw that a recommendation had been made in Congress to elevate the condition of the Indians, in the form of education. About five months since he placed something before Congress, but it was put aside, owing to the agitated state of politics in America. . . ."

KAHKEWAQUONABY: PETER JONES
■

Richard Slotkin, in *Regeneration Through Violence*, writes that the "Indian perceived and alternately envied and feared the sophistication of the white man's religion, customs, and technology, which seemed at times a threat and at times the logical development of the principles of his own society and religion. Each culture viewed the other with mixed feelings of attraction and repulsion, sympathy and antipathy. . . . Once the threat of real Indians was removed from proximity to American civilization and banished to the frontier, the mythicization of the Indian could proceed without the problems and complexities arising from the realities of Indian-white relations. Indian values could be symbolically exaggerated and Indian values accepted as valid for American society, without being rudely checked by some savage outbreak near at hand. The conventional roles of the captivity mythology could even be reversed and the Indians seen as a pathetic alien minority in an 'indigenous' white America. . . . Thus, even as the Indians disappeared from the East, interest in their antiquities and traditions increased. When Indians had abounded, most works dealing with them described them in the context of particular problems. The missionaries discussed their character and religion solely to establish their aptness or inaptness for conversion. . . ."

Monotheism and diseases brought by white men have altered tribal cultures more than any other experiences in the colonial past. Lethal pathogens such as smallpox, bubonic plague, influenza, and other serious infections decimated more than half the population in traditional tribal communities. Missionaries followed the path of death through the tribes, bearing new doctrines that inspired guilt; and the missionaries peddled biblical stories about salvation, transcendence from the pagan woodland to a promised place on the earth, and deliverance from fear and evil. Overwhelmed with sorrow at the muddled fires of religion and colonial expansion, thousands of tribal people were, nonetheless, touched with a new spiritual and evangelical warmth; more were culture burned. Others, like George Copway and Peter Jones, nonesuch tribal people, experienced religious conversion that transformed their personal and public lives. The words and visions of their new religion became the anchor and the storm in their lives, the perfect reason to learn to read and write and to travel as inspired missionaries around the world. In spite of their ecstatic religious rebirth in the language of the colonists, these two tribal missionaries, who became published authors and historical figures with enthusiastic audiences, were critical of federal policies and economic exploitation of tribal resources and cultures.

Peter Jones, for example, writes in his *History of the Ojebway Indians*, that drunkenness, blasphemous words, deception, contagious diseases, and other evils, were all introduced or caused by white people.

"It is painful for me to relate, that of all the children that have been born among those tribes with which I am acquainted, more than one half die before even reaching the period of youth; it is only those who have the strongest constitutions that survive the shocks and exposures to which they are subjected during infancy and childhood. The poor mothers are very ignorant of the nature of the diseases common to children, and of the proper treatment of them; sometimes their clothing is very scanty, at other times they are almost smothered in blankets. The food which they eat is often injurious, and thus disease is generated by the very means used to subdue it. . . . The diseases most common among the aborigines of America before the landing of the Europeans were few, in comparison with those now deliberating their constitutions, and so rapidly thinning their numbers.

"There is a saying among our people, that our forefathers were so exempt from sickness, that, like the cedar which has withstood the storms of many ages, and shows the first signs of decay by the dying of the top branches, so the aged Indian, sinking under the weight of many winters, betokens, by his gray hairs and furrowed cheeks, that life is declining. . . ."

Jones describes in personal metaphors the death of tribal families, but the medicine he prescribes comes from his religious conversion, not from mythic tribal connections in the oral tradition. The evils of the white people, he writes, "can be remedied only the by benign influence of the gospel, the precepts of which teach men to be sober and industrious, to cultivate the earth, and provide for their families. By these means they would soon possess everything necessary for the supply of their temporal wants, and at the same time be inspired with gratitude to the bountiful Giver of all good."

Christian credence and conversions, however, seldom embraced tribal cultures with a sense of human sameness. The tribes were to be saved from their color and ordained cultural inferiorities, delivered as solemn victims to the polished thresholds of the church and the classrooms of colonialism. Tribal people were measured at a distance but seldom admired for their imagination.

Samuel George Morton, for example, a medical doctor and scientist, studied the skulls of various tribal cultures to determine the characteristics of human races. In *Crania Americana*, published in Philadelphia in 1839, Morton concluded that American Indians were deficient in "higher mental powers" because, according to his calculations, the few heads he examined seemed to be smaller than his own. "The benevolent mind may regret the inaptitude of the Indian for civilization. . . ."

Morton writes that tribal people "are not only adverse to the restraints of education, but for the most part are incapable of a continued process of reasoning on abstract subjects. . . . The structure of his mind appears to be different from that of the white man, nor can the two harmonize in the social relations except on the most limited scale. . . ."

Stephen Jay Gould, in *The Mismeasure of Man*, points out that "racial prejudice may be as old as recorded human history, but its biological justification imposed the additional burden of intrinsic inferiority upon despised groups, and precluded redemption by conversion or assimilation. . . ."

Peter Jones, or Kahkewaquonaby in the language of the Anishinaabeg, was born in 1802 in Canada on a tract of land named Burlington Heights. His mother was Anishinaabe; his father was Welsh, a government surveyor. Kahkewaquonaby, which means "sacred feather" in translation, was given his tribal name by his grandfather. "I was named after my mother's brother, who died at the age of seven," Jones writes. "The Indians have but one name, which is derived either from their gods or some circumstance connected with their birth or character. Many of their names are taken from the thunder gods, who, they suppose, exist in the shape of large eagles. . . . These feathers plucked from the eagle represent the plumes of the supposed thunder god, by which it flies from one end of the heavens to the other. When my name was given me, a bunch of eagles' feathers was prepared for the occasion. It was considered sacred, as it represented the speed of the thunder and the eagle.

"A singular fancy prevails among the Ojebways with respect to mentioning their own names. When an Indian is asked his name he will look at some bystander and request him to answer. This reluctance arises from an impression they receive when young, that if they repeat their own names it will prevent their growth, and they will be small in stature. On account of this unwillingness to tell their names, many strangers have fancied that they either have no names or have forgotten them. . . ."

The *History of the Ojebway Indians: With Especial Reference to Their Conversion to Christianity* was published in 1861 by A. W. Bennett in London. The Reverend G. Osborn, Secretary of the Wesleyan Methodist Missionary Society, writes in a letter to the publisher of the posthumous book, that Peter Jones was a man of "sterling piety, with much natural good sense and shrewdness; and had evidently taken great pains in the cultivation and improvement of his mind. His appearances in this country, on two successive visits, afforded high and just gratification to immense numbers of persons, who saw in him an undeniable proof, both of the capacities of his countrymen, and of the power of Christianity to reclaim and elevate those who were at the utmost distance from European civilization. . . ."

Jones, like George Copway twenty years later, visited England. He arrived at Liverpool in April 1831, his first of two visits, and attended missionary meetings in several communities. He preached about his experiences at the King Street Chapel in Bristol. He revealed to the colonists the dark tribal past and his evangelical conversion, and he proposed changes in tribal cultures. James Wood, at whose home the mixed-blood missionary was a guest, noted that Jones became ill during his visit. "He delivered a short and suitable address with great simplicity," Wood writes in a letter. "The audience were much delighted, but expressed great concern to see his debilitated appearance. He remained on the platform about twenty minutes, returned to our house, and the next day took to his bed."

It would be unfair to leap into the past with the accusation that Peter Jones was a sycophant, a person whose manner seldom earns collective favors, but the servile tone of the following letter to Charles Paulett Thomson leaves that impression. The letter to the Governor-General of British North America was signed by Jones, Joseph Sawyer, John Jones, and thirty-six other chiefs from different tribes, nine years after his first visit to England.

"Father . . . We, the Children of the great Mother, the Queen, who sit beyond the great waters, beg leave most respectfully to approach you, our great Father, for the purpose of congratulating you.

"Father . . . We are the original proprietors of this country, on which your white children have built their towns, and cleared their farms.

"Father . . . Our people were once numerous, free, and happy, in the enjoyment of the abundance which our forests, lakes, and rivers produced.

"Father . . . When the white man came into our country, our forefathers took him by the hand, and gave him land on which to pitch his wigwam. Ever since that time he has continued to flow to our shores; and now the white man is greater and stronger than your red children.

"Father . . . For many years we have been made very poor on account of the introduction among us of the firewaters and other evils, which have killed or ruined many of our fathers.

"Father . . . About sixteen years ago the words of the Great Spirit were preached to us by the Methodists. We opened our ears, and the Good Spirit opened our hearts, to receive the Gospel; and we are happy to inform your Excellency that great changes have taken place among our people. We have forsaken our old ways and evil habits, and are trying to live like good Christians and good farmers. We have churches, school-houses, and fields. These things make our hearts very glad.

"Father . . . The presents we receive from our good Mother, the Queen, are of great benefit to us and our people, and we beg to convey to her Majesty, through your Excellency, our unfeigned gratitude for the same, which we hope may ever be continued.

"Father . . . We rejoice to assure your Excellency that we are perfectly satisfied and contented to live under the good and powerful protection of the British Government, who have already proved, by repeated acts of kindness, that they are the true friends of the red man; and we shall ever hold ourselves in readiness to obey the calls of our Great Mother the Queen to defend this country.

"Father . . . We are also glad to state that the fame of British generosity has spread far to the west, and many of our red brethren living within the territory of the United States have experienced a desire to come and settle in the dominions of our great Mother the Queen.

"Father . . . As her Majesty has been pleased to send a chief of our exalted station and wisdom for the purpose of arranging and settling the affairs of these provinces, we lift up our hearts to the Great Spirit above that he may bless your important undertaking, and make you a great blessing both to the white and red men of this country; so that our children after us may rise up and call you blessed.

"Father . . . We now shake hands with you in our hearts, in which all our warriors, women, and children unite.

"This is all we have to say. . . ."

River Credit Mission, 24 January 1840.

Jones had expressed an interest in becoming a federal agent to work with tribal people, but in spite of his achievements and qualifications, he was never offered an appointment. His education, he must have thought, and his religious conversion, would have led to success in the white world. He was disappointed that he was never called on to determine or to administer federal policies for tribal cultures. Jones was misguided, perhaps at the ecstatic intersection of his religious conversion; the white road he followed from the woodland earned him much adulation but few real responsibilities in the world of colonial economics and political institutions. As he celebrated the bent and talent of the church and his spiritual resolutions, Jones seemed to be unsure about his identities as a mixedblood and a missionary. His use of pronouns connotes his personal uncertainties. He writes, for example, that the "intercourse which has long subsisted between the red man and the white man has to a great extent changed the character of the former as regards native simplicity, moral habits, language, and dress. Some of the aged relate that their forefathers informed them that previously to the arrival of the white man in America the Indians were far more virtuous than they are now, and that the fire-waters have tended to demoralize them in every respect. . . ." In an earlier chapter, however, he writes that "it should also be remembered that the pagan ideas of bliss are almost entirely sensual, and relate to the unrestrained indulgence of the animal appetites.

"Alas! they know nothing of that real peace which the world can neither give nor take away. From experience of my early life, I can truly say, that their imaginary bliss is so mixed up with everything that is abominable and cruel, that it would be vain to look for real happiness among savage tribes. . . ."

Jones writes that the Anishinaabeg, "although believers in a future state, know nothing about the blessedness of heaven, as an inheritance procured by the merits and prepared by the grace of the Savior. They have, therefore, no motives to impel them to a life of holy obedience, and to qualify them for the enjoyment of that world of glory. . . . The Indians believe in the existence of the soul after the death of the body, but their ideas on this subject are very confused and absurd. The little knowledge they think they possess is derived from persons who have been in a trance, and travelled in their dreams to the imaginary world of spirits. . . .

"They believe that the souls of brave warriors, good hunters, or the virtuous, and the hospitable, go there and spend an eternity in carnal pleasures, such as feasting, dancing, and the like; but the soul of the coward, the lazy hunter, the stingy, the liar, the thief, the adulterer, and the unmerciful, they imagine will wander about in unknown regions of darkness, and be exposed to the continual rage of wolves, bears, panthers. . . ."

His posthumous book is a personal narrative about the origins of tribal cultures on this continent, anecdotal demographics, and specific cultural characteristics of the Anishinaabeg. Jones writes about courtship and marriage, religion, feasts and sacrifices, war, amusements, diseases, names, culture contact, intoxicants, tribal women and families, language, and educational potential. Jones seldom removes the black robe of religious conversion from his prose; he seldom cracks a verbal smile in his literate memories and moralizations. He survived several epidemics and suffered severe infections, all of which seemed to draw him closer to the promises of a new religion, and, as a result, he was separated from traditional tribal cultures in his narrative posture. He was writing for a white audience; there were few tribal readers in the woodland to review his descriptions of their culture. Jones generalized tribal traditions and experiences and for the most part he expressed the familiar romantic and racist notions common in the white world.

"Of all the causes which have contributed to the rapid decrease of the Indian tribes, the abuse of ardent spirits, while following their native mode of life, is, in my opinion, the primary and most important. For when an Indian is intoxicated, all the savage passions of his nature assume the entire control, often leading him to commit the most barbarous acts of cruelty and even murder. . . ."

Jones, who was a missionary in the Wesleyan Methodist Church, mirrored the critical views of the white temperance movement: he emphasized the evils of alcohol in tribal cultures, when he could have observed that some tribal cultures and families refused to be abused by alcohol. The Presbyterian Church inspired the temperance movement, which, in the beginning, was "not a prohibitionist crusade," but a doctrine of moderation, except where tribal people were involved. Mark Lender and James Martin, in *Drinking in America*, point out that in 1816 the "Methodists pledged to redouble their temperance efforts, and their ministers spread the gospel" that hard liquor posed "moral and social threats. . . ."

Jones separates himself from his past in most of his references to tribal culture and behavior. He writes that "their indolence leads them to be very improvident; the thought of laying up a store of provisions beforehand seems never to enter their minds; but so long as they have anything to eat, they will lounge about and sleep, and never think of hunting till hunger presses them to go in search of game. They spend their time when in their villages or wigwams, in smoking, making their implements of war and hunting, and talking over their various exploits in the chase and in the flight. To strangers they are reserved, but among themselves they are notorious talkers and newsmongers; no event occurs in any village but it is soon published abroad. In the presence of others they are seldom known to hold any conversations with their wives. . . .

"In accordance with the custom of all pagan nations, the Indian men look upon their women as an inferior race of beings, created for their use and convenience. They therefore treat them as menials, and impose on them all the drudgeries of a savage life. . . . Indian women, notwithstanding all the heavy burdens imposed on them, are generally true and constant in their affections to their husbands. No mothers can be fonder of their children, though some may think they are destitute of natural love. This mistake has arisen from the fact that some of the *drunken* Indian women have been known to sell their children for a bottle of whiskey, or suffered them to perish for want of proper attention and care. . . .

"Any remarkable features in natural scenery or terrific places become objects of superstitious dread and veneration, from the idea that they are the abodes of gods: for instance, curious trees, rocks, islands, mountains, caves, or waterfalls. Whenever they approach these it is with the greatest solemnity, smoking a pipe, and leaving a little tobacco as an offering to the presiding spirit of the hallowed spot. . . . They consider the thunder to be a god in the shape of a large eagle that feeds on serpents, which it takes from under the earth and the trunks of hollow trees. When a thunderbolt strikes a tree or the ground, they fancy that the thunder has shot his fiery arrow at a serpent and caught it away in the twinkling of an eye. Some Indians affirm that they have seen the serpent taken up by the thunder into the clouds. . . ."

Animosh, or the feast of the dogs, is "considered a meritorious sacrifice," he writes. "After the dog is killed and the hair singed off, it is cooked among the guests, a portion being devoted as a burnt offering. The dog is considered by Indians as an ominous animal, and supposed to possess great virtue. . . ."

Jones concludes his book with stories and anecdotes about religious conversions, although he does not reveal the detail of his own conversion. He writes that "John Caleb, an Indian youth at Muncey Town, when about twelve years of age, was converted to the Christian religion, and became very anxious to learn to read and write. He was much opposed by his parents, who were heathens, and threatened to take his gun and horse and sell them for the fire-waters, if he did not give up going to the meetings and school. John told his parents that he thought more about serving the Great Spirit than he did about the gun or his horse, and would therefore rather lose all he possessed than give up his school and religious meetings; and more than this, he modestly told them he would rather suffer death than disobey what the Great Spirit had commanded him to do. John then prayed earnestly for the conversion of his parents, and that good Being who hears and answers the prayers of faith gave him the desires of his heart in their sound conversion. Let young persons never be discouraged; God will surely answer their prayers, if offered up in sincerity and faith. . . ."

Jones, or his publisher, included an excerpt of a letter from Joseph Rucky, or Oshenahwageshiek, who wrote to the tribal missionary on January 8, 1852:

"I am wishing to come to your school, Muncey Town, if possible. I have been to school here, Wesleyan Seminary, Albion, but my time will be out next spring. My people are very poor, and have not the means to assist me. I belong to the Chippewa tribe. Half of us are in Canada, and the remainder, to whom I belong, are in Michigan. I wish to know if you could assist me to come to school, as it would enable me to instruct our ignorant brethren. I wish to have a little more instruction in the English language. I know you can assist me anywhere to go in your schools. I would endeavor to make it a lasting benefit to our poor people, by teaching them the way of life. Please send me an answer.

"Yours truly. . . ."

The Reverend Peter Jones died at age fifty-four after a long illness. "Sinking under excessive attacks of disease," the grave marker reads in part, "caused by exposures and labours in the Missionary work, he died, triumphing in the faith which he preached during his memorable ministry of thirty-one years in the Wesleyan Methodist Church."

OLD CROW WING TO WHITE EARTH

■

Subjectivism is the ultimate loneliness. Symptoms of it have appeared in the past, but they seem far more prevalent in modern times. With people of preliterate and traditional societies, reality is given. . . . Indeed nature itself, under questioning, dissolves into subjective experience.

Yi-Fu Tuan
Segmented Worlds and Self

■

OLD CROW WING
■

Julia Spears moved from Madeline Island to the Chippewa Agency near Crow Wing in Minnesota. She was a widow with three children, and a government day school teacher, when the White Earth Reservation was established more than a century ago. "It was a year after the treaty," she remembered in a letter about her experience, "before all the Indians could be persuaded to leave their old home."

The Younger Hole-in-the-day and other leaders of the Anishinaabeg, who were identified by public officials as the Mississippi Band of Chippewas, negotiated with the federal government to establish a new larger reservation in exchange for their smaller reservations, which had been created in earlier treaties. The Younger took the name of his father Hole-in-the-day (a descriptive name in translation), who was born during an eclipse.

"Hole-in-the-day became dissatisfied and unruly," Julia Spears wrote. "He demanded much for himself as chief which was refused by the government. He then began to oppose the removal and made much trouble by trying to prevent the other chiefs and braves from starting, telling them to wait until next spring as he would not be ready until then. . . ."

75

He demanded that the government improve the new reservation, including a sawmill, tribal housing, and other personal amenities and tribal betterments. Hole-in-the-day told federal officials that "when all these improvements were made he would be ready to go. The agent had received orders from the department to have the Indians removed to their new homes early that spring, and they were all ready to start. Hole-in-the-day was very angry when he found that he could not prevent them from moving, and threatened to kill the first to go. Some of his braves supported him in his stand."

D. B. Herriman, the Indian agent at the Chippewa Agency, seemed to admire Hole-in-the-day as a farmer. In his annual report to the commissioner he wrote that the "leading chief has set them a laudable example in farming; near the agency a piece of land, containing about sixty acres, had been broken and partially fenced; upon this piece of land, after his return from Washington, he resolved to work, and with such industry and perseverence did he labor, that during the payment he was enabled to sell to the Indians between two and three hundred dollars worth of vegetables, besides having sufficient for winter's use for his own family, and oats and hay for his stock. . . ."

Herriman, who did not praise tribal intellectual development, argued that tribal people should be removed from small communities to one large reservation, where each person would receive a garden plot to begin the transformation from hunter to farmer. "One, and perhaps the greatest, hindrance to the advancement of the Indians in civilization," the agent writes in his annual report, "is the frequent changes in general policy pursued toward them by the government; the frequent removals that have heretofore been required of them have retarded very much their advancement; allowing large sums of money yearly, to employ a number of mechanics at one agency, has tended to confirm the Indian in his naturally indolent habits. The system of education generally practiced among the Indian tribes, educating them from books, rather than in the workshops, has been a source of evil rather than good."

George Kerr, in a personal account of old Crow Wing, wrote that Hole-in-the-day, who had ceded a large tract of land near Leech Lake to the federal government, was killed "by the Pillager Indians. His body had lain there for some time before it was found. It was brought back to Crow Wing and buried in an unmarked grave near the mission church."

"There is an old story that was told about the time" Hole-in-the-day returned from a meeting with federal officials, and "with his white wife that he got twenty-thousand dollars in gold—that is why" other tribal members "all wanted a split. They claimed he buried it near his house. . . .

I have heard this had something to do with his murder. People around here also believe it. Some believe it to this day. When I was a boy, two men at the Crow Wing station asked me if I knew where the Hole-in-the-day house was. I told them, 'yes.' They gave me some loose change to show them where it was. I think I got fifty cents in all which I thought was a lot. They had a team of horses and a buckboard buggy. We started out across the prairie toward the location. The man driving the team said to the older man, 'how far will your dip needle attract anything like that?' He answered, 'about twenty rods.' He said to me, 'how far are we from the spot?' I told him it was about a quarter of a mile from there. The driver told the older fellow to get his dip needle out. Sure enough, he got an attraction right away. . . . Every summer there were people looking for the money but the venture always ended in failure." No gold was ever found.

"Finally, after much trouble," Julia Spears remembered, the removal began on June 4, 1868, to the White Earth Reservation. That fall, the first annuities, ten dollars a head, were paid to those tribal people who had moved to the new reservation in the woodland.

Crow Wing was a trading post and village at the confluence of the Mississippi and Crow Wing rivers. Allan Morrison and Clement Beaulieu were the prominent traders in the area. Beaulieu, who was born at Lac du Flambeau in Michigan Territory, the mixedblood son of Basile Hudon dit Beaulieu and Ogemaugeezhigoqua, associated with numerous influential people in the fur trade. He proposed a townsite on the shores of the two rivers where the first railroad line was expected to be built, but his friends from the fur trade were not able to influence the expansion of new economics in the state. The Northern Pacific Railroad was built north of Crow Wing, and when businesses moved to the new station at Brainerd, the scenic and historic settlement near the Crow Wing and Mississippi rivers declined. Beaulieu, whose trading license had been suspended, was removed to the White Earth Reservation with other mixedbloods from small tribal communities in the area.

"I am expecting an easy time this summer if my health should be as good as it has been for some months past," wrote Elizabeth Ayer in a letter to her son. She was the first school teacher at old Crow Wing. "Expect to have not more than twelve pupils. . . .

"Crow Wing is quite dilapidated. The Beaulieu house in which so many gentlemen of rank, and ladies too, have been entertained is empty; the yard fence is much broken and hogs and other animals have destroyed what they can that is valuable on the premises. Surely, 'Things have an end.' "

WHITE EARTH RESERVATION
■

The mixedblood editor and publisher of *The Progress*, the first newspaper published on the White Earth Reservation, announced in the first issue, dated March 25, 1886, that the "novelty of a newspaper published upon this reservation may cause many to be wary in their support, and this from a fear that it may be revolutionary in character. . . . We shall aim to advocate constantly and withhold reserve, what in our view, and in the view of the leading minds upon this reservation, is the best for the interests of its residents. And not only for their interests, but those of the tribe wherever they now are residing.

"The main consideration in this advocacy will be the political interests, that is, in matters relative to us and to the Government of the United States. We shall not antagonize the Government, nor act, in the presentation of our views, in any way outside of written or moral law.

"We intend that this journal shall be the mouth-piece of the community in making known abroad and at home what is for the best interests of the tribe. It is not always possible to reach the fountain head through subordinates, it is not always possible to appeal to the moral sentiment of the country through these sources, or by communication through the general press. . . .

"We may be called upon at times to criticize individuals and laws, but we shall aim to do so in a spirit of kindness and justice. Believing that the 'freedom of the press' will be guarded as sacredly by the Government on this reservation as elsewhere, we launch forth our little craft, appealing to the authorities that be, at home, at the seat of government, to the community, to give us moral support, for in this way only can we reach the standard set forth at our mast-head," which dedicates *The Progress* to "A higher Civilization: The Maintenance of Law and Order."

Following the publication of the first issue of *The Progress*, federal agents confiscated the press and ordered the removal of Theodore Hudon Beaulieu, the editor, and Augustus Hudon Beaulieu, the publisher, both of whom were tribal members, from the White Earth Reservation. The second issue of the first newspaper on the reservation was published about six months later, when a federal district court ruled that *The Progress* could be published without government interference.

T. J. Sheehan, the malevolent United States Indian Agent on the White Earth Reservation, forbade the publication of the newspaper five days before the first issue was released. Sheehan, who seemed to be obsessed as much with form and politics as with editorial content, wrote

Office of *The Tomahawk*,
White Earth Reservation,
about 1910. Photo courtesy
of Minnesota Historical
Society. *The Progress* became
The Tomahawk about the turn
of the century.

to the editor and publisher that they had "circulated a newspaper without first obtaining authority or license so to do from the honorable Secretary of the Interior, honorable Commissioner of Indian Affairs, or myself as United States Indian Agent. . . ." Sheehan asserted in his formal letter that Augustus H. Beaulieu "did scheme and intrigue with certain chiefs on White Earth Reservation without the knowledge of myself and the Indians of this agency, for the said chiefs to proceed to Saint Paul, Minnesota, for the purpose of signing a power of attorney for the Mississippi Indians, deputizing a person to act as an attorney for the Indians in certain business interests affecting the welfare of the Indians on White Earth Agency, all of which I consider revolutionary to the United States Government and a detriment to the welfare of these Indians. . . .

"Whereas, you have at different times advised the full and mixedblood Indians to organize and 'kick' against the rule established by myself as United States Indian agent, for the suppression of card playing, or other games which may be detrimental for the Indians on this agency, in either the hotels or store-buildings of White Earth Reservation. . . .

"Whereas, Theodore H. Beaulieu has written and caused to be printed in a newspaper adjacent to White Earth Reservation, false and malicious statements concerning the affairs of the White Earth Reservation, done evidently for the purpose of breaking down the influence of the United States Indian agent with the Indians of White Earth Agency. . . .

"For the above reasons," and more, the agent stopped the publication of the newspaper for about six months. Sheehan, however, continued his harassment of those who disagreed with his capricious decisions. Frequent complaints from tribal people brought about an official investigation of the conduct of the agent on the reservation. Notwithstanding the interests of the Committee on Indian Affairs of the United States Senate, which convened about a year after the first issue of *The Progress* was published, and the reports from hundreds of hearings since then, the abuses of authority by federal agents have continued on reservations.

Clement Hudon Beaulieu was the first witness who testified before the Subcommittee of the Committee on Indian Affairs. The clerk marked the time of the meeting, Tuesday morning, March 8, 1887, on his calendar. Senator Morgan examined several letters before him, then he cleared his throat and asked the first question:

What is your age?

I was seventy-five years old last September.

What family have you living with you?

I have my wife living with me. . . .

Is your wife Indian or white? asked Senator Morgan.

She is half Chippewa and half Scotch.

Are you Chippewa?

Yes, sir, responded Clement Beaulieu.

Full blood?

No, sir; half French and half Chippewa, Beaulieu explained.

What other members of your family have you living in the house?

My children are all grown up; there is only one living with me. My oldest son, Charles Beaulieu, has been in the Army.

Which Army?

The Union Army. In 1862 I raised up a company for him of mixed-blood, Indians and French. I got him a hundred men.

And he took them into the Army?

Yes, sir.

He was a captain of the company?

Yes, sir; he was captain of the company. . . .

What children have you living in the house with you?

Press room of *The Tomahawk*,
White Earth Reservation,
about 1902. Photo courtesy
of Minnesota Historical
Society.

Theodore, one of my youngest sons. . . .
Where do you reside?
I reside at the White Earth Agency.
How long have you lived there?
For fifteen years. . . .
What other sons have you?
I have another, a minister. This one is forty-seven years old, the oldest, and the other one is about forty-nine. He is a minister. . . .
Where does this minister reside?
He is now in Mason City, Iowa.
What church is he minister of? asked Senator Morgan.
The Episcopal Church, answered Beaulieu.
How long has he been in that calling?
He was confirmed about four or five years ago.
What is your religion?
Catholic; we are all Catholics except that one.

Your wife is a Catholic?

Yes, sir. . . .

Have you any daughters?

One.

Is she married?

Yes, sir.

What is her name?

Julia Beaulieu. She is married to one of our relatives of some distance.

A cousin, I suppose?

Yes, sir; a second cousin.

What is her husband's name?

Theodore H. Beaulieu.

So that he has the same name of your son?

No, sir; the other one is Theodore B. Beaulieu, and this one is Theodore H. Beaulieu, responded Clement Beaulieu.

How much of a family has Julia?

She has had three children.

Where do they live?

They live about a mile from me, from the town.

On the reservation?

Yes, sir; on the reservation. . . .

What order has been made by the Secretary of the Interior in regard to the removal of your family or your daughter's family? asked Senator Morgan.

The only way we can tell there is to be a removal is by the letters of the Secretary of the Interior to the agent, Clement Beaulieu responded.

Does that include your wives and children?

No, sir; only ourselves alone.

So that you are to be banished from that country and separated from your families.

Yes, sir, both; as long as this order continues. The agent asks for us to be permanently removed forever. I have not seen it myself.

Other persons have seen the order of removal, but you have never seen it?

No, sir; I have not seen it.

Have you or your son-in-law, Theodore H. Beaulieu, the means to break up at the reservation and go elsewhere with your families and make a support?

I do not know whether it will come to that. . . .

But have you the means to leave?

No, sir; we have no means at all. . . .

So that if you are compelled to remove your families from the reser-

Chief White Cloud, White
Earth Reservation, about
1890. Photo courtesy of Minnesota Historical Society.

vation it will amount to the destruction of all you have earned in your life?

Yes, sir; the whole of it. . . .

Are you a citizen of the United States?

I was born in what is now the State of Wisconsin, said Clement Beaulieu. My mother was a member of the Chippewa tribe, and my father was a Frenchman. I was born before any treaty was made between the Chippewas and the United States. The first treaty was made in 1837. No removal of the Indians was made to any tract, but they ceded our land to us. No reservation was made, but we had a right to occupy the land and to hunt as usual. . . .

When did you move to Minnesota?

I was two years in Canada and in 1838 I came to Wisconsin and have remained there just on the edge of Minnesota ever since until 1846, and then I removed as an agent for the American Fur Company to Minnesota. . . .

When did you first join the body of Indians of which you are now a member, the White Earth Indians?

I joined them under the treaty of 1854, when there was a separation between the Lake Superior Indians and the Mississippi Chippewas. I joined that band because I could not go so far back as Lake Flambeau. Under the provisions of that treaty we were allowed to go either with the Mississippi Chippewas or with the Lake Flambeau Indians, and they would be considered as the Lake Superior Chippewas, and from that time I have always been with the Chippewas of the Mississippi.

Have you ever been a voter?

I have, Clement Beaulieu responded. I voted in Crow Wing County, Minnesota, near Brainerd—about twelve miles from Brainerd. . . .

Was this voting done under the laws of the State of Minnesota?

I don't know whether it was or not, but I was allowed to vote.

You thought it was under the laws of Minnesota?

We thought it was, because it was outside the reservation. We did not see anything to prevent us. I don't know whether it was done to get the votes of the half-breeds.

But all the half-breeds outside the reservation voted?

Yes, sir. . . .

Did you muster with the militia?

No, sir; but when Mr. Sibley was governor he appointed me lieutenant-colonel in the State militia, and that is the reason they call me colonel now.

Have you held office and paid taxes?

Yes, sir. . . .

Where was that?

That was in Duluth.

In what county?

We had no county established at that time. . . .

Under what law did you do all these things?

I thought I had the law of Minnesota, or Wisconsin as it was then, to go by . . . the law of the Territory. I had a few pieces of the printed laws; I do not know where I picked them up or whether they were the laws of Michigan or Wisconsin, and I used them to dictate to me what to do. But it was all a mistake, I suppose. . . .

What was your reason for wanting all this power?

To keep the peace; that was the only motive.

Was there much trouble with the Indians up there?

There was a good deal of stealing.

And you wanted to prevent that?

Yes, sir. . . .

Are your children educated people? asked Senator Morgan.

My children pass to be educated. They are the best educated boys, I think, there on the reservation, my boys are.

Where did you educate them?

When I was at Brainerd . . . I sent for a teacher and kept him there as long as I could, and then sent them down to Saint Paul, and then, after they were there, I thought they hadn't enough, hadn't but a small education, and I sent them down to New Jersey and kept them there as long as I could.

All of your children?

No, sir; four of them. The other one didn't want to be educated, he wanted to be a farmer, and I could not get him to go away from home. . . .

Is your daughter educated?

Yes, sir; I sent her to a convent and I gave her all the education in music and everything, responded Clement Beaulieu.

How many Indians now, about, belong to the White Earth Reservation?

Altogether I think there are are between seventeen hundred and eighteen hundred of the Mississippi, Otter Tail, and Pembina bands. . . .

What is the general condition of the people in the Chippewa country now in regard to food? asked Senator Morgan.

We get along well enough with the mixed-bloods, but the full-bloods are suffering. . . . An order was issued . . . to furnish seed to the Indians, and if there was a surplus to give it to the mixed-blood people. Instead of that they commenced with the mixed-bloods, who had plenty of grain for farming, and the Indians afterwards got behind, and could not get what seed they wanted to fill up their farms.

I take it, from what you say, that the mixed-bloods are a little sharper people than the native Indians?

They get on with their work better, and they understand it. An Indian does not understand it . . . it takes them some time; but they see they cannot make their living in any other way than out of the soil; there is no more game. . . .

Are there any mills in the White Earth Reservation?

We have no mills now; we had a mill, but that has been condemned. . . .

How far do the Indians have to go to get their milling done?

They go about eight miles, but, then, that man has cheated them very much, explained Clement Beaulieu. . . .

What is your observation as to the amount of drinking that is carried on in that White Earth Reservation, so far as your knowledge extends? asked Senator Morgan.

Anishinaabeg from White
Earth Reservation, at
Hallock, about 1895. Photo
courtesy Hudson's Bay
Company.

Well, there has been a good deal last winter, more than usual. . . .
The Indians go out and get whiskey and bring it in?

Yes, sir; and have a good spree in the night time. Sometimes a man
will be caught up in the day-time and he will be taken up, but they are
very careful.

When an Indian wants to go off the reservation to have his wheat
ground or to traffic in any way at all, if I understand you, it is not usual
for him to get any pass or consent whatever?

No, sir; he goes along without asking anybody about it.

When you came here to Washington you did not get permission from
anybody to come?

No, sir; no permission; I just started and came along. . . .

Clement Beaulieu was questioned further about food supplies, game
and fish, maple sugar and wild rice, and the attitudes and behavior of
federal agents and missionaries toward the mixedbloods and the publication of a newspaper on the reservation. A letter, signed by more than
two dozen tribal leaders, including White Cloud, Ignatius Hole-in-the-
day, Wahjimah, Wahmegons, Mahjikeshig, Nahtanub, and others who
worked on the reservation, was entered in the official subcommittee
transcript of the Committee on Indian Affairs. The letter denounced the
charges against Clement Hudon Beaulieu and Theodore Hudon Beaulieu

as "false and malicious . . . and we cheerfully bear testimony to their ability and unblemished character. . . ."

John Johnson Enmegahbowh, the tribal missionary who established Saint Columba Church at White Earth, wrote to the committee that he knew Clement Beaulieu to be "always upright and honorable and zealous in the civilization and advancement of his tribe." Enmegahbowh, the tribal son of trappers, was ordained an Episcopal priest by Bishop Henry Whipple. His letter is significant in view of the struggles between the Episcopal and Catholic missions on the White Earth Reservation. Clement Beaulieu and his family, with the exception of his one son, were members of the Catholic Church. The Episcopal missionaries, for the most part, were critical of the influence of the mixedbloods on the reservation and supported most of the accusations made by the federal agent.

Indian agents were the colonial agents for the federal government on reservations. Their appointments in most cases were political favors, and their practices on reservations were seldom viewed as honorable by tribal members. T. J. Sheehan, for example, attempted to remove tribal mixedbloods from the reservation because they were determined to express their views; he ordered the newspaper closed and the presses removed; and he interpreted federal policies capriciously, in favor of his own interests, inhibitions, and personal philosophies. Sheehan did not limit his rancor to tribal people and mixedbloods; he accused James Woodward, a medical doctor, of causing problems on the reservation. Sheehan wrote to the commissioner that the doctor permitted "dancing, drinking, and carousing in a new building lately built for the physician on the reservation, causing the building to settle, breaking and cracking the plastering, and breaking down one of the doors to a room in the building. . . . I would most respectfully request that he be dismissed from the service or removed from the reservation. . . ."

Doctor Woodward told the committee that he never danced in the building against the orders of the federal agent; he explained that "on one occasion he did forbid my dancing, and I had the dance in a house opposite my residence, as I understood the order applied to that particular time and was not a general order that I should never dance in the house. Also that I only on one occasion had three quadrilles, or there were three quadrilles danced on one evening, and that the couples dancing the said quadrilles did not leave the floor, and that Agent Sheehan was not absent from the reservation at that time. . . ."

What was it that occurred which caused Agent Sheehan to bring these charges against you, so late after that occurrence? asked Senator Morgan.

Well, sir, Doctor Woodward responded, I believe it was on account of this ill-feeling or disturbance between the Beaulieus and Agent Sheehan, and from the fact that I did not side in with the agent, but sympathized with the Beaulieus, that he concluded that I was undermining him, and doing everything in my power to injure him. . . .

Have you ever seen any misconduct on the part of any of the Beaulieus at that agency or in that Territory?

Not on the part of either or any of those whom he has made charges against, responded Doctor Woodward. I once saw a younger member of the family under the influence of liquor; not that he was boisterous or in any way ungentlemanly, but he was slightly under the influence of liquor. . . .

Senator Morgan seemed preoccupied with racial measures of civilization in his questions. He asked various witnesses about their education, and about mixedblood attitudes toward agriculture and their work habits. He implied in his persistent questions about reservation manners that civilization, because of race, was more obvious in mixedbloods. At the turn of the last century, the prevailing public attitude, supported by several scientific studies, was that tribal cultures were inferior, savage or primitive. It was believed then that tribal people and their cultures would vanish either by death from diseases or alcoholism, or by mixedblood assimilation into the dominant culture. Federal policies encouraged the elimination of tribal cultures; on most reservations tribal languages, religious practices, even ceremonial and social dances, were forbidden. When the tribes vanished, according to racist assumptions, reservation land would revert to the federal government, notwithstanding several hundred treaties.

Richard Drinnon, in *Facing West: The Metaphysics of Indian-Hating and Empire-Building*, argues that in the "national experience race has always been of greater importance than class. . . . Racism defined natives as nonpersons within the settlement culture and was in a real sense the enabling experience of the rising American empire: Indian-hating identified the dark others that white settlers were not and must not under any circumstances become, and it helped them wrest a continent and more from the hands of these native caretakers of the lands."

Did you have a dance after that? asked Senator Morgan.

No, sir; we had no dance at the house, replied Doctor Woodward at the hearing. We danced at a house opposite and had the supper at our own residence. . . .

Are the Beaulieus educated people?

Yes, sir; they are refined and educated people.

Have they decent, nice houses to live in?

Yes, sir.

How about the furniture—are their houses well furnished?

Their houses are comfortably furnished.

Are they considered respectable people in the community?

To my personal knowledge, and from statements made to me by people who have known them from thirty to fifty years, who give them the best kind of character, I can say they are, responded Doctor Woodward. . . .

Are they supporters of law, order, and Christianity, or are they outbreakers and violent people? asked Senator Morgan.

I never have known them to commit any deeds of violence or to try to excite any outbreak or anything of the kind on the agency there.

Does old man Beaulieu enjoy the respect of the people of that community?

Yes, sir; he does.

Is he a man of influence there?

He is a man of a great deal of influence in his tribe. He has always taken a leading part in anything which would be of benefit to his tribe, and has advised them to cultivate industry and the habits of agriculture, and try and advance themselves in civilization.

Has he been prominent and decided in that line of action?

Yes, sir. . . .

What is you idea of Sheehan's conduct as an agent, whether he is a dutiful and competent man or whether he is negligent in the performance of his duties?

I consider that he is thoroughly incompetent and unfitted for the position of agent, responded Doctor Woodward.

Why is he incompetent; what is the difficulty?

In the first place he lacks education, and he lacks executive ability. . . .

Is he competent to take charge of the books of the agency, asked Senator Morgan, and see that they are correctly kept?

No, sir.

Is he an illiterate man?

Yes, sir; he is an illiterate man; his early education has been sadly neglected, in my opinion, the doctor answered. . . .

Agent Sheehan considered the educational policies on the reservation to be a success. In his annual report, submitted in the same year as the committee inquired into his affairs, he writes that the "schools under my charge within the White Earth Agency, under the peculiar circumstances by which they were surrounded, in the occasional appearance of measles, which depopulated the schools at various times, were in the end a success. The overseers, teachers, and all other persons connected with the schools deserve great credit for their laudable tenacity in keeping their schools running with such an average attendance under such a trying ordeal. . . . In connection with the work of education I have constantly kept in view the two great elements or principles underlying Indian civilization, which are education and agriculture, for while the Indian youth's head needs training, his hands need it more. With all the book-learning he may obtain, unless he has been taught to handle a plow, shove the plane, or strike an anvil, he is as helpless as a child when thrown out into active life." Elizabeth Bella Beaulieu and Julia Warren were assistant teachers at the White Earth Boarding School that year; their annual salaries were four hundred and eighty dollars each.

Sheehan concludes, in his uncommon style, that "Peace, quiet, and harmony prevail among the Indians within the limits of this agency. The progress made during the past year by the Indians on this reservation . . . is a good and substantial proof of their honesty of purpose and determination to do and achieve for themselves the blessings of a permanent home. My corps of employees at the present time are efficient and satisfactory to me, and I take pleasure in stating that their cordial support and manly co-operation have been of great help to me in the performance of my official duties. . . ." The agent, whom Doctor Woodward described as being "illiterate," did not mention in his annual report to the commissioner that he had forbidden the publication of a newspaper on the reservation. Sheehan, it seems, was more interested in the abilities to shove a plane or strike an anvil than he was in literature and the publication of a newspaper. The newspaper must have been a double threat: the agent was suspicious of educated mixedbloods, and he was sensitive to the public evaluation of his policies and administration of the reservation.

Clement Hudon Beaulieu was recalled as a witness on Friday, March 11, 1887, by the Subcommittee of the Senate Committee on Indian Affairs. Senator Morgan continued his examination into the affairs at the White Earth Reservation.

Have you any ill feeling towards the Government of the United States?

No, sir; but against the officers. . . .

Is your ill feeling towards them on your own personal account or because you have found fault with their administration of affairs connected with the Indians?

It is because of their administration of affairs connected with the Indians, responded Clement Beaulieu, and not allowing them to have it investigated. . . .

Your idea was that the Indians ought to have something to do with the administration of justice in their own reservation?

Yes, sir; so that we can be forming a kind of government as we go along.

Do you think the Chippewas are as competent to have a local government as the Cherokees? asked Senator Morgan.

Yes, sir; I think so, especially as we have so many educated half-breeds who can take the lead, explained Clement Beaulieu.

The half-breeds are educated men?

Yes, sir; we have quite a number of them who are well educated.

If you cannot get that sort of government are you willing to go under the government of the State of Minnesota?

That would be just right so far as the half-breeds are concerned, but it would be too hard for the full-bloods, I think, for the present. . . .

Your idea was that to bring the wild Indians in amongst the civilized Indians would tend to civilize the wild Indians and not harm the others?

That was my idea. We have so many of the half-breeds there that I was perfectly sure we could bring this about. The half-breeds are my strength, and I depend on them to help bring about civilization.

You still believe that if these full-blooded Indians were brought in there and distributed around through the reservation, that the influence of the educated half-breeds would civilize them and cause them and their children to become educated?

Yes, sir, responded Clement Beaulieu. . . .

You have a post-office at the White Earth Agency?

Yes, sir.

Do the mails run regularly to that post-office?

Yes, sir.

Do they bring letters and papers from any part of the United States without restriction? asked Senator Morgan.

Yes, sir.

Newspapers printed in other parts of the United States are brought there and circulated amongst the Indians?

Yes, sir; there are a great many subscribers to newspapers there.

Has there been any effort to prevent the circulation of newspapers by the authorities there amongst the Indians?

Not that I know of, responded Clement Beaulieu.

Have you heard of any newspaper published in the United States being sent there and suppressed or the circulation of it not allowed?

No, sir.

Does the paper called *The Council Fire* circulate there?

Yes, sir.

That is an Indian paper?

Yes, sir.

Doesn't that paper contain pretty severe strictures upon the administration of Indian affairs? asked Senator Morgan.

Yes, sir. . . .

Do the papers which go there have free comments upon Indian agents. . . ?

Yes, sir.

You have heard of no suppression of those?

No, sir; not one.

The Progress was first published on March 25, 1886, at the White Earth Reservation. Six months later on October 8, 1887, the second issue of the idealistic newspaper was published following an official government investigation and a court hearing.

Theodore Hudon Beaulieu, the editor, wrote the following on the front page of the second issue of the newspaper: "In the month of March last year, we began setting the type for the first number of *The Progress* and were almost ready to go to press, when our sanctum was invaded by T. J. Sheehan, the United States Indian Agent, accompanied by a posse of the Indian police. The composing stick was removed from our hands, our property seized, and ourselves forbidden to proceed with the publication of the journal. We had, prior to this time, been personally served with a written notice from Mr. Sheehan detailing at length, surmises beyond number as to the character of *The Progress*, together with gratuitous assumptions as to our moral unfitness to be upon the reservation, charging the publisher with the voicing of incendiary and revolutionary sentiments at various times.

"We did not believe that any earthly power had the right to interfere with us as members of the Chippewa tribe, and at the White Earth Reservation, while peacefully pursuing the occupation we had chosen. We did not believe there existed a law which should prescribe for us the occupation we should follow. We knew of no law which could compel us to become agriculturists, professionals, 'hewers of wood and drawers of water,' or per contra, could restrain us from engaging in these occupations. Therefore we respectfully declined obeying the mandate, at the same time reaching the conclusion that should we be restrained we should appeal to the courts for protection.

"We were restrained and a guard set over our property. We sought

SAMPLE COPY

MINNESOTA HISTORICAL SOCIETY.

OJIBWA FOLK LORE! THIS WEEK. Historical, Traditional, Legendary and Entertaining.

THE PROGRESS.

LOOK OUT! —FOR— Wainnahboozho

"A higher Civilization: The Maintenance of Law and Order."

VOL. 1. WHITE EARTH AGENCY, MINNESOTA, SATURDAY, DECEMBER 17, 1887. NO. 11.

The Progress.

Gus. H. Beaulieu, - - Publisher.
Theo. H. Beaulieu, - - Editor.

White Earth Agency, Minn.

A WEEKLY NEWSPAPER devoted to the interest of the White Earth Reservation and general Northwestern News. Published and managed by members of the Reservation.

Correspondence bearing on the Indian question—problem, or on general interest, is solicited.

Subscription rates: $2.00 per annum. For the convenience of those who may feel unable to pay for the paper yearly or who may wish to take it on trial, subscriptions may be sent us for six and three months at the yearly rates. All subscriptions or sums sent to us should be forwarded by Registered letter to insure safety.

Address all communications to
THE PROGRESS.
White Earth, Minn.

TIME TIME, SEMI TIME, TIME TIME.
FRANK M. HUME,
DETROIT, MINNESOTA.
—DEALER IN—
Clocks, Watches and Jewelry.
REPAIRING A SPECIALTY.
WHITE EARTH Orders, if left with Benjamin Caswell, at Fairbanks & Bro.' Store will receive prompt attention. 4tf

—HOTEL—
HINDQUARTERS.
Ed. Oliver, Proprietor.
Everything in first class keeping with the times.
The tables are always provided with Fish, Game and Vegetables in their season. Good stabling, ample accommodation for both, man and beast.
BOARD BY THE DAY OR WEEK.

R. FAIRBANKS.
Dealer in
GROCERIES
PROVISION.
and
Lumbermen's Supplies.
FLOUR and FEED kept on hand.
Ginseng, Snake Root and Furs Bought, Sold and Exchanged.

THE PROGRESS
JOB
WORK
—AND—
Printing
Establishment.
All kinds of Job Printing, such as Bill Heads, Letter Heads, Blanks, Cards, Tags etc., solicited.
Work Warranted and Satisfaction Guaranteed.

(Copyright.)

The Ojibwas.

THEIR CUSTOMS AND TRADITIONS,

As Handed Down for Centuries, From Father to Son. etc., etc.

By BAY-BODGE.

Grand Sachem and Medicine Seer of the White Earth Ojibwas, now about 90 Years of Age.

ORIGIN OF THE INDIANS.

My grandson you have asked me to tell you the customs of our ancestors and the origin of the Indians. It is your wish and I shall tell you our beliefs.

The first appearance of the Unish-in-ab-baig (human beings or Indians) occurred in this way:

When the Gitche-Manito (Great-Spirit) made up his mind to create man, He took a handful of earth and rubbed it together in his palms and behold a man was formed! The Spirit below the Earth, who was a very Imposing or Grand Spirit, with heavy locks of white hair, said to Kitche-Manito in counsel, "What are You going to do with only one Indian?" In answer to this question, Kitche-Manito took another handful of earth and rubbed it in his palms and behold a woman was formed, and He said, "this person shall be the fruit of the earth, and the seed from which shall come the Indian race;" this my grandson, is how the Indians originated and became so numerous.

NAMING THE CHILDREN.

I shall now tell you our customs regarding the naming of children, and customs by which their lives are guided thereafter. It is believed every child, while it is in its mother's womb, wonders in this way: what disposition its parents are going to make of it. When a child is about to be born its parents commence to accumulate provision and clothing. After its birth this provision is used for a feast by the parents. A spokesman is selected by the father who is supposed to act for the child; a meeting of some of the principal men of the tribe or band is held, and it is decided who shall be the namesake, or rather whose body to whom the child is dedicated. It does not necessarily follow that the child shall be named after that particular person, but he must in the course of time give it some name.

When the selection of a Ne-ah-wa-ain (after my body) is made, the spokesman who has been selected to preside over the meeting, now invokes the Great Spirit to guard the future of the child and give it a long lease of life, etc. During this prayer a pipe with a long decorated stem is lit, and offered as a sacrifice to the Great Spirit. The stem is first pointed to the East, South, West, North and then downwards, towards the Earth. After this ceremony is concluded, the person who has been selected to name a child is called in and informed of the duty imposed upon him, and he accepts by saying Ho!—Amen. A nickname is generally given to a child however, by the parents or some other relative of the child, but its real name is given only by its Ne-ah-wa-ain, which is usually done when the child is first sick.

My grandson, it was the custom of our ancestors to be guided throughout their lives by their dreams, and with some of those dreams he is deeply impressed, and it was this class of dreams which guided our ancestors. An Indian during his life very often dreams of all kinds of animals, birds and other objects, and some one of these impresses him deeply. A person who is selected to name a child, tells it of some dream in which a certain animal or object figured, and says, "Ne-ah-wa-ain will be named after it, and I will go after the animal which I have told you about." His main object then is to procure the animal etc., he may have dreamed of, which the Great Spirit usually allowed him to secure; after which it is cooked and served out at a grand feast in which the friends and relatives participated. The dedicatee then commences a chant, which has been composed by him for the occasion, and of words which he had at sometime during his life dreamed of. The animal which has been cooked is a peace offering to the Great Spirit by the person who named the child, because he (god-father) dreamed of this and knew how to conciliate the Great Spirit who permitted the child to be born and allowed it to live. The Great Spirit very seldom takes the child away because He pities the Indian who has confidence in him. This my grandson, was the way our ancestors named their children.

GIRLHOOD TO MAIDENHOOD.

Bah-cah-ne-gay, or Bay-cah-nish-co-dah-way (different lodge, or different fire) was a custom followed by the women of the Ojibwa tribe, and was established among them by an Indian of whom I will have much to say later, and whose name was WAIN-NAH-BOO-ZHO. It will take a long time to tell about him as all our traditions refers to him. When the Earth was covered with water he was the being who formed a new one. But I will not speak of him to-day. It was of the custom regarding women of which I am going to speak. My grandson, you see by the locks of my hair, which have been whitened by the snows of many winters that I am a very aged man, and many, many moons ago the custom which I intend to speak of, was followed by our women. Since the old men of our tribe have all dropped away, and disappeared from the earth, and especially within a few years, you never hear that a young girl who has just reached puberty is removed or sent away from an Indian village, that is, during the time Nature is changing her from childhood to womanhood, neither do you ever hear of a 'different fire' or a 'different lodge' for a woman now. But in those days our women had strong restrictions placed over them.

When a young girl first became aware of the change Nature was about to make with her, she immediately left the village to which she belonged, and built at some distance away from it a small wigwam, of a sufficient size to allow her to lie down comfortable, but not high enough to stand in it. She then remained in this temporary lodge as long as she could fast, which was from five to ten days. She would not go any distance from her lodge, for if a man crossed her tracks while she was undergoing the transition referred to, he immediately fell to the ground paralyzed, and it became necessary for the medicine men to be called in to cure him. My grandson, you cannot properly understand without an illustration, how strong a spirit for good or evil a girl is during this period. When I was a young man I had many warts on my hands, in fact they were almost covered by them, and the old women of my tribe advised me to go to a girl who had built a 'bay-cah-ne-gay' at some distance from our village, and who was undergoing the fasting period, and have her cure me. I disliked the warts very much, and being ashamed of my ugly looking hands, I reluctantly concluded to follow their advise. I was warned about 'crossing her tracks,' and to approach the lodge from the side very carefully, and if I reached it safely to pass my hands in to her from the sides of the lodge and say, "I have come to you to cure my hands!" I approached the lodge, passed my hands in, and repeated the words as directed. She wet her fingers with her saliva and touched all the warts on my hands, and when she had completed this I retraced my steps, and returned to the village. In five days all the warts on my hand had disappeared.

While a girl is passing this period she eats nothing of her own volition, and not until her mother offers her something, which must be a piece of fresh meat cooked almost to a crisp over living coals of fire. She will not accept this if she can forego the temptation, for the longer she fasts the more she can see of her future life by dreaming. If a girl fasts ten days it is supposed to cover the whole period of her life. During this time she does not only go without food, but also without water. It is during this time also that she learns whether the Great Spirit will accept her as a Medicine woman, and if He does she composes songs which she is to sing when she becomes such. I had omitted to say also, a young girl had to wear mittens on her hands and a cloth or hood on the head to cover her hair, as we believe that if a girl touched her hair with bare hands their growth would be stunted and remain short forever. A woman with short hair is a disgrace and an object of contempt among our people.

BOYHOOD AND MANHOOD,—LEGEND OF THE ROBIN.

When young men reached manhood they selected the longest days in the year, which was generally late in the spring, and wandered away from the villages to which they belonged, into the lonely forest and where they would proceed to build a nest in some tree and in which they would lie down and commence their fasts, which usually lasted from five to ten days without food or water. During these fasts they had many dreams, and by those dreams the course of their future life were guided, both on the war-path and in their hunts.

A young man once wandered from his tribe in the Spring time to undergo the customary fast. After he had fasted for several

[CONTINUED NEXT WEEK.]

The Indian; Right and Wrong.

"We hold these truths to be self-evident, that ALL MEN are created equal; that they are endowed by their Creator with certain unalienable rights; that among these, are LIFE, LIBERTY, AND THE PURSUIT OF HAPPINESS."—Declaration of Independence, July 4th, 1776.

PREJUDICIAL VAGARIES!.

It seems uncreditable that such abortive assumption of prejudicial sentimentality on an imagineary conception of a state of existing conditions, as is porported in the following article from the Duluth Herald in refference to the Red Lake reservation, should be indulged in by the journalists of today, and is befitting only the cheap vaporing of the writers of "dime novels," etc. We reproduce it in the columns of The Progress to give its readers an opportunity of judging how little some people really know of what they talk and write about at times; and that after all, when such gush is boiled down, one can not fail to discern midst the dregs, the conclusive motor of this 'wishy-washy' hellabelloo of 'murderers, loafers, pirates, thieves, etc., is simply used to guard the frantic efforts of the ghouls and vultures of outright robbery and fraud, swayed by the ignominious spirit of greed and gain! The thousands of acres of land, the millions of feet of pine timber, etc.,—there's the rub, that's the eyesore of the hordes of unfeeling vampires who are endeavoring by fair or foul means to get the "lion's share" of this "Redskin Alsatia."

A Refuge of Murderers and Outlaws—A Redskin Alsatia.

The murder of Israel Ryder, the wellknown fur trader of Rosseau lake, near the Red Lake reservation is a sample of the crimes that these pets of the Eastern philanthropists are constantly committing. A grand farce of sending a bishop and some other folks to make treaties with these Indians, was indulged in last summer. The press was deluged with slush about the good bishop praying for the satety of birch canoes, etc. The Indians were praised as being industrious, and in fact the whole repertoire of Boston Indianidiocy was worked for all it was worth. to those who know these Indians, the habits, manners and customs, this gush is simply sickening. These worthy bishop and treaty makers would hold up their hands in "holy horror and pious grief" if they only knew that all the talk given them by the Indians was just so much "guff." Indians have a profound contempt for all whitemen. They fear them it is true, but an Injun is an Injun clear through, and when he gets a chance, he will never fail to do a white man up. The Indians upon the Red Lake reservation are a very bad lot. So are the Pillagers, and the Bois Forte bands, at Net Lake, near Vermilion, and not far behind in the procession. Red Lake is a reliable redskin "Alsatia." It was there that the notorious Riel took refuge after the first Red River rebellion. When an Indian commits an outrage upon the Rainy River settlers or lumbermen he crosses the river and snaps his fingers in derison at the law. This reservation is also overrun with those pests of the frontier, the squawmen. The degraded wretches, "white-Indians" as they are generally called, are ten times meaner than the meanest Injun on the reservation. It is largely due to these men, that alcohol is easy to be obtained by the Indians. Every trader upon and around the Red Lake reservation is a whiskey dealer, and even the autocratic and dignified Hudson Bay company was not slow to send its rum to the fur hunters of Red Lake. There are thousands of acres of splendid timber lands and farming lands within the boundaries of this reservation that are now simply used as a resort for murderers, loafers, whikey pirates, and fur thieves. This state of things will continue just as long as the sickish sentimentality in regard to the Indians is kept up. If the United States government really desires to benefit the Indians, let them be given citizen's rights, and left to sink or swim with the rest. This petting and coddling of full grown men is ridiculous. An average Indian is no born fool, and is better fitted by nature to take care of himself than nine white men out of ten. Give the Indian the same chance as the European peasant immigrant and he will probably be just as able to keep his end of the log at a reasonable altitude. One thing is certain, an Indian would never become an anarchist.

LEECY and McARTHUR,
—DEALERS IN—
GENERAL MERCHANDISE,
LAKESIDE AVENUE, ... WHITE EARTH, Minn.

G. A. FAIRBANKS & BRO.,
—GENERAL DEALERS IN—
Dry Goods, Groceries, Hardware,
Farming Implements and Lumbermen's Supplies.
COR. LAKESIDE AVE. AND SELKIRK STREET. WHITE EARTH, Minn.

the protection of the courts, notwithstanding the assertion of the agent, that there could be no jurisdiction in the matter.

"The United States district court, Judge Nelson in session, decided that we were entitled to the jurisdiction we sought. The case came before him, on jury trial. The court asserted and defended the right of any member of a tribe to print and publish a newspaper upon his reservation just as he might engage in any other lawful occupation, and without surveillance and restrictions. The jury before whom the amount of damage came, while not adjudging the amount asked for, did assess and decree a damage with a verdict restoring to us our plant. . . .

"Now that we are once more at sea, fumigated and out of quarantine, and we issue from dry dock with prow and hull steel-clad tempered with truth and justice, and with our clearance registered, we once more box our compass, invite you all aboard, and we will clear port, set sails to favorable breezes, with the assurance that we will spare no pains in guiding you to a 'higher' civilization."

The Progress was not the first newspaper to be published on a reservation, but it was the first tribal newspaper to be seized by federal agents. *The Progress* was published for two years and then the newspaper was enlarged and the name was changed to *The Tomahawk*. The editor and publisher remained the same; both newspapers published reservation, state, and national news stories, and controversial editorials. In addition to information about tribal cultures and government policies, the newspapers on the White Earth Reservation opposed the federal legislation that allotted collective tribal land to individuals. One article, for example, carried the following headline over a two-column front page report: "Is it an Indian Bureau? About some of the freaks in the employ of the Indian Service whose actions are a disgrace to the nation and a curse to the cause of justice. Putrescent through the spoils system." Almost a century later, leaders of the American Indian Movement used similar language in criticism of the Bureau of Indian Affairs.

In the past decade, thousands of periodic newsletters and newspapers have been published in tribal communities and on reservations. The circulation of these newsletters and newspapers is often small, but the number of publications on reservations indicates a need among tribal people for more news and information by and about themselves. The several newsletters published on the six reservations in the state merged to become one large subscription newspaper. *Speaking of Ourselves* is published by the Minnesota Chippewa Tribe and contains original news stories and articles reprinted from other newspapers. Betty Blue, editor of *Speaking of Ourselves*, wrote in a recent issue about the problems of ter-

THE TOMAHAWK.
"Truth before Favor."

VOL. 1. WHITE EARTH, BECKER COUNTY, MINNESOTA, TUESDAY, JUNE 16, 1903. NO. 12.

The TOMAHAWK.

GUS. H. BEAULIEU - - Publisher.

White Earth Agency, Minn.

A WEEKLY Newspaper devoted to the interests of the White Earth Reservation and general Northwestern News. Published and managed by members of the Reservation.

Subscription rates: $1.50 per annum. For the convenience of those who may feel unable to pay for the paper yearly or who wish to take it on trial, subscription may be sent us for six and three months at the yearly rates. All sums sent to us should be forwarded by registered letter to insure safety. Address all communications to.

THE TOMAHAWK,
WHITE EARTH, MINN.

RESERVATION LANDS TO LEASE

100,000 acres of first class farm lands on White Earth Reservation, in tracts of 80 acres and more, by ALLOTTEES.

INDIAN PROTECTIVE Association
200 Bond Building
Washington D. C.

Seq'l B. Henderson, Att'y.

Indian claims against the United States a speciality.

K. S. MURCHISON,
ATTORNEY AT LAW.
LATE LAW CLERK, LAND DIVISION, INDIAN OFFICE.
DEPARTMENT PRACTICE A SPECIALTY.

LOAN AND TRUST BLDG.
WASHINGTON D. C.

Hotel Leecy.
White Earth, Minn.

The Largest and Most Commodious Hotel on the Reservation.

Table always bountifully supplied with everything that the market affords, including game and fish in season.

A large and comfortable, Feed and Livery stable in connection with Hotel.

JOHN LEECY Prop.

Selam Fairbanks,
Dealer in
DRY GOODS,
GROCERIES,
HARDWARE
and
Lumbermen - - Supplies.

Market price paid for Ginding Snake Root and Furs.

Orders for pure Maple syrup, and wild rice promptly attended to.

BEAULIEU - - MINN.

"The Tomahawk."

TRIAL Subscriptions.

3 months . . . . . . 40 Cents
6 months . . . . . . 75 Cents

THE WHITE EARTH RESERVATION.

Brief History of Events Which Lead to Its Establishment.

Under a misapprehension which extended among the Pillager Chippewas, Hole-in-the-day, the celebrated chief, forfeited his life.

Without going into the details of the causes which led to the uprising among the Chippewas in 1862, we will merely state that there was sufficient provocation in the minds of the Indians to enable the late celebrated chief, Hole-in-the-day, to induce them to take up arms against the government.

Although Hole-in-the-Day has always been charged with being the instigator of the uprising, it is certain that he did not commence hostilities until an attempt was made by army officers to arrest him.

The first intimation the public got that the Chippewas contemplated an outbreak was when Lieut. Forbes, now a resident of Albert Lea, with a squad of soldiers, made an attempt to arrest Hole-

Hole-in-the-day.

in-the-day at the old village of Crow Wing.

But the writer hereof, who was then a boy of nine years of age, met Hole-in-the-day and his escort or hears Quayte-good, a short distance from th village, and upon being questioned by the chief, told him that the soldiers were at Crow Wing. Quay-te-good ha proceeded on his way without stopping and when Hole-in-the-day got through conversing with us, he went to the hill overlooking the village, and from ther saw the soldiers arresting the former But the soldiers also got sight of him and immediately started to pursuit him. He took a trail near the river which led to his house, and which once the distance nearly one mile nearer than by the wagon road, and he succeeded in reaching home, and removing his family to a place of safety before the soldiers arrived there. When the latter got to the house they saw Hole-in-the-day crossing the Mississippi river in his private ferry boat. They rushed to the river bank and got there just as the boat touched the opposite shore. Lieut Cake, however, got the impression tha they had been over-reached in the matter of the treaty of 1867, and held Hole-in-the-day responsible for it. .

Hole-in-the-day fired his revolver and returned the shots, gave a war-whoop, and disappeared over a hill Within a minute after that he returned to

C. H. Beaulieu, who took an active part to suppress the outbreak, and brought the Mille Lac Indians to come to Ft. Ripley in 1862.

Crow Wing

with a large form of braves, and surrounded the town.

The commissioner of Indian affairs who happened to be there, held a peace council with the chiefs, but without any results. A short time after the Dul council, Gov. Ramsey, who had strong influence over the Indians and especially over Hole-in-the- . . . arrived a Crow Wing and succeeded in inducing the braules to disband and return to their respective reservations. The action of the Mille Lac Chippewas, who had tendered their services to the government to suppress the uprising, contributed largely to the cessation of hostilities by Hole-in-the-day.

Three hundred commissioners by th Chippewas led to the treaty of March 11 1863, wherein the Mississippi Chippewas ceded six reservations in this state in lieu of a large tract of land which now known as the Mississippi Chippewa reservation, within which the Leech, Cass and Winnebegoish lake are located, with the view of being consolidated thereon.

This treaty, which was made a Washington, by the chiefs of the several lands of Chippewas in Minnesota caused so much dissatisfaction amon the Indians that another delegation went to Washington in 1864 and succeeded in making another treaty on May 7 that year, which greatly increased the size of the reservation set aside by the treaty of the previous year. Several years after the treaty of 1864, it was found that the Mississippi reservation

White Cloud, who was one of the chiefs that made the treaty of 1868.

was not adapted to farming purposes and in 1867 Hole-in-the-day was author ed by his band to proceed to Wash ington and there negotiate another trea y. On March 19, 1867, the treaty setting aside thirty-six townships of land as to include the White Earth and Wild Rice lakes, was concluded.

No definite boundaries being fixed b the treaty, Hole-in-the-day, Major Jo D. Bassett, who was then the United States Indian agent for the Chippewas, and Paul H. Beaulieu, selected the reservation and fixed, approximately, th boundary lines thereof. The wisdom o this selection can never be questioned since the reservation is now considere the garden spot of Minnesota.

Assassination of Hole-in-the-day.

The Pillager Chippewas of Leec Lake, however, got the impression tha they had been over-reached in the matter of the treaty of 1867, and held Hol in-the-day responsible for it. .

Peter Roy, who acted as one of the interpreters of the treaty of 1868.

The ill-feeling on this account was very bitter against him among them, and in August, 1868, a party of nine of them, headed by May-dwa-we-nind, one of the leaders of the Leech Lake uprising in 1898, started for the old Chippewa agency, near Crow Wing, intent doing in the part.

which

Hole-in-the-day was living, for the purpose of assassinating him. When they arrived at his house they did not find him there, he being absent at Crow Wing, where he was making preparations to start for Washington on the following day.

They then decided, after discussing the matter, to go to Crow Wing, and there wait an opportunity to kill him. They immediately started for that town, and when they were about one mile from the agency they met Hole-in-the-day in his buggy, with Chief Ojibway of the reservation, and just after he had passed them, May-dwa-we-nind shot him in the neck, killing him instantly.

Gull Lake Indians Start For White Earth.

Three months prior to Hole-in-the-lay's assassination, Paul H. Beaulieu started for this reservation with the first contingent of Mississippi Indians from the Gull Lake reservation, near Crow Wing. They were en route sixteen or seventeen days, and on the 14th day of June, 1868, they arrived at the

Paul H. Beaulieu, who led the Chippewas to white Earth Reservation in 1868.

ld trading post, two miles from here. The conditions which confronted the settlers upon their arrival here were uch that it was a very difficult task for the officials to induce them to remain here. And notwithstanding the efforts to keep them here, many of them returned to their homes at Gull Lake, and it was only within a few years issued that they were induced to return here.

It was not until 1871, when E. P. Smith the first Indian agent that was appointed under President Grant's famous peace policy, that any further effort was made to remove the Indians of the Mississippi lands to this reservation.

Immediately after Mr. Smith took harge of the White Earth Indian agency, he succeeded in having the appropriations made which were provided by treaties, and in less than two years had started the removal of a large number of Indians; and, by his policy of dealing with and encouraging them, induced more half-breed Indians to open farms than all the agents here have since

THE GOVERNOR'S PARTY.

At one o'clock yesterday Governor Van Sant and party arriv at this Agency. They were met several miles from here by the . dian police force, chief Me-sha-ke-shig and others, all mounted, w acted as an escort from there to the Agency.

The party consists of Governor and Mrs. Van Sant, United Stat district attorney and Mrs. C. C. Haupt, Miss Haupt, assistant Unit State's district attorney J. M. Dickey, Mrs. Rogers, Mr. Best, repre sentative of the Minneapolis Times and George Van Smith, represen ative of the St. Paul Globe.

Chief Mesha Kegwahig, who participated in the negotiations of th treaties of 1863 and 1864, and who, although over seventy years o age, is taking an active part in the present celebration here.

Prominent Indians who took part in the anniversary celebration here, on June, 15 and 14. 1902

PROGRAMME

First Day, Monday, June 16th.

Federal Salute at Sunrise.
Exercises of the Day to commence at 8 o'clock A. M.
Grand Aboriginal Parade. - The Indian of Yesterday.
Music by the White Earth School Military Band.
Vocal - National Anthem.
Music by White Earth Cornet Band.
Speeches by Hon. Ray W. Jones, Lieut.-Gov. of Minnesota; Hon.
M. J. Daly, of Perham and Chief Joseph Charrette.
Music by the Band.

DINNER.

Music by White Earth School Military Band.
Indian Games and races:
Aboriginal and Bowery Dancing:
Game of Base Ball between the Rice River and the
White Earth nines.
Matinee in the Assembly Hall, Subject—Longfellow's "Hiawatha"
by Native Men and Women.

A TWO HUNDRED YEARS WAR.

A majority of our visitors here today attending the celebration doubtless know that the Sioux and Chippewa Indians carried on a fierce and relentless war against each other for two hundred years and more, but we doubt if many of them know the causes which led up to this war.

There are two versions of the causes of the war given by the Chippewas. One of them is to the effect that there was a large settlement of Chippewas at the mouth of the Wisconsin River, and an equally large settlement or village of Sioux, three or four miles up the River from the Chippewa settlement; that during the spawning season each year the Chippewas built a dam near the mouth of the river, so as to prevent the fish from going up the river. The Sioux resented this and demanded that the dam be removed, which the Chippewas refused to do. At soon as the Chippewas refused and resisted by the Sioux chief, he gathered his forces and started for the dam with the view of destroying it. But the Chippewas hearing of this awaited the arrival of the Sioux forces, and when the latter attempted to break the dam a pitched battle took place and the long war followed, and Chippewa villages were located at the points named.

The other version, which is more romantic, is that the Sioux, and that the son of the Chippewa chief was an accepted suitor of a beautiful Sioux maiden. The maiden also had another suitor among the members of her own tribe, who one evening met the Chippewa, rival, and without any warning shot him in the back with an arrow, killing him almost instantly.

The Chippewas made a demand upon the Sioux to surrender the murderer, and upon their refusal to deliver him to them, the Chief formed a war party, and charged on the Sioux village and almost exterminated the Sioux that were living there.

While both of these versions are plausible, it is generally believed among the Indians that the war was commenced at the point indicated.

Rev. J. J. Inine-me-gubow, who inaugurated the 14th of June celebrations.

succeeded in doing. While the progress of the Indian as farmers has been very slow and unsatisfactory to the government, there are a great many of the members of this reservation who have from one hundred to five hundred acres of land under cultivation on their farms.

Prospective railroads through this reservation will be an inducement here after for the reservation farmers to enlarge their farms, since the prospects of being able to sell their farm products at railroad stations will be equally as good as to haul this produce from twenty to thirty miles as they have been doing in the past.

mination: "What is the ultimate Indian nightmare? If you said 'termination,' you'd probably be right. So when Interior Secretary James Watt told viewers of 'Conservative Counterpoint' that Indian reservations . . . should be 'set free' it was natural that Indian leaders would perceive in this the suggestion that tribes be cut from their unique ties with the United States government. . . ."

Several tribal newspapers appeal to a national audience and have national circulation. *Wassaja*, first issued about sixty years ago in Chicago by Doctor Carlos Montezuma, was published a second time by the American Indian Historical Society in San Francisco and became, for a time, one of the most ambitious and successful newspapers published by and for tribal people. Other major tribal newspapers include the *Navajo Times*, the *Tundra Times*, the *Lakota Times*, and *Akwesasne Notes*. All four of these have national circulation. This is not the first time in tribal histories that several important newspapers have been published on reservations. More than a century ago, more than a dozen tribal newspapers were published on reservations from Minnesota to Oklahoma. The *Cherokee Advocate*, for example, was first published in 1843 in Tahlequah, Oklahoma, which was then known as Indian Territory. The newspaper was published in both English and the Cherokee syllabic written language.

Other tribal newspapers of the time, which were published in Indian Territory, include the *Indian Arrow*, published at Fort Gibson; the *Chickasaw Enterprise*, published at Paul's Valley; *Our Brother in Red*, published in Muskogee; and the *Indian Citizen*, published at Atoka. James Melvin Lee wrote in his *History of American Journalism* that another tribal journal, *The Vindicator*, published for the Choctaws and Chickasaws, later merged with the *Oklahoma Star*. In his history of newspapers and journalism, Frank Luther Mott wrote that "since whites could not own land in Oklahoma until after the opening in 1889, the papers published in the territory were designed chiefly for Indians. . . ." The *American Newspaper Directory* for 1888 entered the following for *The Progress:* "The only paper outside of the Indian Territory published and edited by Indians. A true friend of the Indian and his cause. The champion of the coming citizen and a fearless exponent of truth and justice."

Following the last gust of tribal publications a century ago, the federal government enacted land allotment legislation and policies of assimilation. Forced assimilation, however, has never been a successful program. Reservations still flourish; tribal land claims have been received with favor in federal and state courts in the past decade; and there are more tribal publications demanding recognition of tribal sovereignties. Although in the past tribal news was limited to the media of print, tribal owned and operated radio and television stations now exist on several reservations. Migizi Communications, for example, is a national tribal news service located in Minneapolis that produces news and information radio programs for subscribers.

The Circle, February 1984, an urban tribal newspaper published monthly by the Minneapolis American Indian Center.

Boarding School Remembrance

The transvaluation of roles that turns the despised and oppressed into symbols of salvation and rebirth is nothing new in the history of human culture, but when it occurs, it is an indication of a new cultural direction, perhaps of a deep cultural revolution.

Robert Bellah,
The Broken Covenant

WINDMILL AT THE FEDERAL SCHOOL

Wayquahgishig, like many other tribal children, was forced to attend a federal boarding school hundreds of miles from his woodland home, separated from his friends and families, where he was given the name John Rogers and taught that his traditional tribal culture was inferior, even pagan and irrelevant. Rogers is an unusual person, not because he learned to read and write under dominant cultural duress—thousands of tribal children have survived cultural disunities in federal and mission boarding schools—but because he used his new language to write a sensitive book about his experiences on the White Earth Reservation, where he was born at the turn of the last century, about the same time as the tribal newspaper *The Progress* was published on the reservation.

Rogers attended a boarding school for six years. He writes in *Red World and White: Memories of a Chippewa Boyhood* that when he returned to the reservation from the federal boarding school at Flandreau, South Dakota, he found that his parents were separated and his mother was living alone in a wigwam.

"I was anxious to see my mother and be home again," Rogers remembers. "Mother was seated on the ground working on some fish nets. . . . As she stood up with outstretched arms her eyes sparkled as does the sun on laughing waters. . . ."

Notwithstanding his adverse experiences in a racist world, Rogers writes with a sense of peace about the changes he observed in his woodland culture and on the reservation when he returned. He is suspicious at times, dubious of the promises made by white people, but his published remembrance is not bitter or consumed with hatred for white people and their institutions. Rather, he made positive uses of his boarding school experiences and seems to approach the world with a sense of adventure. His brothers and sisters had also been forced to attend boarding schools.

"She started talking joyously, but we couldn't understand very well what she said," Rogers wrote about his mother, "for we had forgotten much of the Indian language during our six years away from home. . . . During the days that followed we had a happy time getting acquainted after those long years of separation. . . . I was pleased to feel that I would grow into a strong young brave, and so I tried very hard to please her and to learn once more the Chippewa language.

"Mother promised to teach me the ways of the forest, rivers and lakes—how to set rabbit snares and deadfalls, how to trap for wolves and other wild animals that roamed this land. . . . Soon came the time for the leaves to turn brown and yellow and gold. The forest was beautiful and the wind rustled the dry leaves. We just couldn't resist the temptation to gather those beautiful colored leaves and the empty bird nests.

"At school, if we brought in a nest or a pretty leaf, we were given much credit, and we thought we would also please mother by bringing some to her. But she did not like our doing this. She would scold and correct us and tell us we were destroying something—that the nests were the homes of the birds, and the leaves were the beauty of the forest."

Rogers expresses a love for nature without philosophical hesitation. His thought rhythms are gentle, and his woodland metaphors are simple and direct. "I had learned to love the primitive life which had for so many, many generations influenced and shaped the existence of my ancestors. . . . Nothing the white man could teach me would take the place of what I was learning from the forest, the lakes and the river.

"I could read more in the swaying of the trees and the way they spread their branches and leaned to the wind than I could read in any books that they had at school. I could learn much more from the smiling, rippling waters and from the moss and flowers than from anything the teachers could tell me about such matters. I could gain knowledge from my daily walks under the trees where the shadows mixed with the shifting sunlight and the wind fanned my cheek with its gentle caress or made me bend, as it did the trees, to its mighty blasts."

Rogers praised nature as a spiritual teacher, and his resistance to the

Anishinaabeg women, about
1945. Photo courtesy of
Minnesota Historical Society.

formulas of institutional knowledge is not unlike the conflicts voiced by
tribal people today. The differences are in personal experiences. Three
generations in the past the author was living two lives in two real worlds,
the last of a traditional tribal culture and a new literate world located in
the printed word. Today, many urban tribal people who have not lived
in the woodland seem to express romantic instincts, dreams and visions
of the wilderness, rather than the metaphors that come from personal
lived experiences. The conflicts have changed in time and place, from
the reservation to the urban world, and so has the language of the past,
and the memories of cultural survival.

Rogers reveals with the insight of a poet the contrasts and contradictions in his experiences on the White Earth Reservation at the turn of
the century. For example, while he was at boarding school, he was appointed to climb to the top of the water tower and oil the gears of the
windmill. "As I stood there breathing hard from my climb upwards," he
remembers, "I noticed how some trees were taller than others. And then
I knew for the first time how the forest and fields and lakes looked to
the bird that sailed so freely and happily about. . . . Looking down again

on the school grounds, the children appeared like dolls as they walked along the paths or ran about at play.

"As I observed these things, I did not, for a moment, regret my leaving the forest home. . . . Perhaps there were advantages that would make up for what I had left behind!" The author is no idealogue; he whispers to the reader at times but he never lectures. His memories seem to unfold like secrets in the oral tradition, not the secrets of a victim or a conspirator, but mythic secrets that abound in nature and in the human spirit.

HOG CART AT THE MISSION SCHOOL
■

A ride on the old hog cart down the hill from the mission boarding school was a memorable experience. Maggie Hanks remembered the ride when she was a student on the reservation at the turn of the century. As a child she first attended the federal school; when the building burned she moved to the White Earth Catholic boarding school, where she made her first communion.

Sister Carol Berg interviewed Maggie Hanks on the reservation and writes in her dissertation, "Climbing Learners' Hill: Benedictines at White Earth 1878-1945," that "she also remembers learning to knit and crochet, nothing that she and her classmates did well enough to be able to have their work exhibited at fairs."

Alice Clark, who was a student at the mission boarding school, also remembered the hog cart ride down the hill. Seventy years later she could repeat the processional lyrics which the students chanted as they moved in columns to and from the school building:

We are climbing learners' hill,
March along, march along,
We are climbing learners' hill,
March along, march along.
We are climbing learners' hill,
We're climbing with a will,
We are climbing learners' hill,
March along, march along.

Rose Shingobe Barstow, who taught in the Department of American Indian Studies at the University of Minnesota, told Sister Carol Berg that she remembered the boarding school with some sadness but with no bitterness. "As early as the third grade, Rose decided to keep quiet in school, fearful of making mistakes and being laughed at by either students or teachers. She remembers another little girl making a mistake in her use of English and being ridiculed for it. . . . The English language was difficult to learn. . . . Rose often practiced her sounds while in bed or any other place where she could be alone."

Rose told about how shocked she was to see tribal people for the first time illustrated in a history book when she was at the boarding school. "Indians were depicted as savages, brutally assaulting some white people. Rose says she studied that picture for a long time," Sister Carol Berg writes, "and recalls that Sister Lioba came along and said, 'You know, *you* are an Indian.' Rose denied this most vehemently at the time but Sister Lioba insisted it was true. Rose asked her grandfather if she were really Indian. . . . Rose's grandfather was a major influence in her formative years. She says, 'I learned to cope with two cultures and I learned to respect other denominations through my grandfather.' Rose credits her grandfather with having taught her a deep respect and toleration for diversity. . . .

"Asked to describe what the mission school did for her in the long run, Rose says the school aimed at giving a general education. The sisters taught basic skills. . . . Rose recalls that the curriculum focused on reading, writing, arithmetic with a heavy concentration also on catechism and bible history. . . .

"Her amusement still evident, Rose told of a small deception played with the collaboration of Sisters Thea and Ethelbert. Rose's father regularly sent fifteen dollars a quarter for piano lessons but Rose did not care to take them. She let another girl take the lessons in her place. A skill Rose did care for and excelled at was that of crocheting. For three and a half years she worked at crocheting an altar lace, seventeen feet long, which was later used for the first time at a solemn High Mass. Since she was supposed to 'preserve' her hands, Rose was not allowed to do the usual chores other students did at the time. . . .

"There were some unpleasant times at the mission school. Rose shared two negative encounters with one of the sisters who was 'different from the rest of the sisters.' When she was in the sixth grade, Rose was accused by this sister of stealing a sugar cake and was whipped with a strap. Rose cried as she sat on the 'punish bench.' Father Valerian, the pastor, came along and asked what was wrong. After further questioning, he got the truth that another girl had done the stealing. Rose still sounds indignant that the sister never apologized for her false accusation. . . . Rose still considers herself fortunate to have had teachers from two cultures and learned equal respect for both."

Father Aloysius Hermanutz, one of the first missionaries at White Earth, delivered colonial and monotheistic tokens of assimilation to the tribal people on the reservation. He was born in Germany and ordained two years before he arrived in the woodland, at age twenty-three, to begin his dedicated conversion of tribal dreams and oral traditions. Sister Carol Berg, in her article, "Agents of Cultural Change: The Benedictines at White Earth," published in *Minnesota History*, quotes from the notes of Father Aloysius: "We made no wholesale conversions among the Indians, such as we read of being made in Asia and elsewhere. Soul after soul had to be gained by hard fight, patience and prayer, and many of these were converted from their heathen views and practices only after years of hard work. . . . The largest number baptized by me on one day was seventy, and this after a preparation of one week with the help of four catechists."

Sister Carol Berg points out that tribal languages were not taught in the mission school on the reservation. Several missionaries, however, learned a few words and phrases, enough to communicate their compassion in the native language of the children and their families. "During their many years at White Earth," Sister Carol Berg concludes, the pioneer "Benedictine missionaries grew to know and respect some aspects of Ojibway culture, but their own goals, like those of most of their fellow Americans working with Indian people, were directed strongly toward change. Perhaps if they had been introduced to Indian traditional religion and culture, if they had had a sense of their own positions as agents of cultural change, and if they had considered the idea of missionary adaptation to Indian culture as well as to the ideals and aims of Indian mission work, the process of change might have been different for both the Ojibway and the missionaries."

Sister Mary Degel taught first and second grade at the mission boarding school. She remembers "being bothered at first by the fact that she was warned not to get too familiar with the girls," according to Sister Carol Berg, who interviewed her when she retired. "She was criticized for being too lenient with them. But there were many runaways, and Sister Mary thinks the schedule at White Earth was too rigid for the girls — especially for those who were delinquents brought there by social welfare workers as a last chance before being taken to a corrections institution. . . ."

Sister Carol Berg asked her about her impressions of tribal cultural traits in the children. "She says she found them affectionate, good-natured, and a happy people. She cited as basic for success in working with them an understanding of Indian background and being honest with them. Indians are quick to detect deceit. . . . 'They are suspicious due to hard raps, but if they trust you, they are very loyal.' "

Father Benno Watrin has been a priest for more than half a century, working most of the time with tribal people. For seventeen years he was a pastor at Ponsford on the White Earth Reservation. Sister Carol Berg reports that she asked him about his "opinion of Indians before and during the time he was a missionary. . . . He admitted that he had not thought very much of the Indian culture, feeling it inferior to his own. 'I was a simple farmer boy and I thought ours was the only way to live.' Yet, he tried to speak Ojibwa whenever possible, rather than insisting on having English for the services. . . . I was impressed that he can still rattle off sentences in Ojibwa and knows the Our Father in its entirety in that language. . . . Father Benno was most distressed over how few Indians came to church regularly. Ricing and berry-picking kept them away, he says."

Julia Spears, who had been a teacher in the government school at Crow Wing, moved to White Earth two years after the reservation was created in 1868 and opened the first school. There were forty students in her first class on the new reservation. The following year the federal government established an industrial boarding school. "During the year 1873 the government buildings were completed," Julia Spears writes in a letter, "including the large school-house and boys' building, also the industrial hall where the Indian women were taught housework, including cooking, sewing, knitting, carpet-weaving," and other domestic abilities and trappings of a dominant white culture.

Nine years later, a church and school were built by Catholic Benedictine missionaries with money from St. John's Abbey in Collegeville, Minnesota, and according to Sister Carol Berg, "with a small donation from the Ludwig Missionsverein of Munich, Bavaria. The new convent-school building could accommodate twenty orphans. Classrooms, for both day students and boarders, were located in the church basement. However, the expanded space was insufficient for all the children whose parents wished to send them to the mission school."

Most of the children who attended the mission boarding schools were under government contract requiring that the school provide subsistence and medical care. "A further regulation," Sister Carol Berg points out in her dissertation, "which caused a strain on the White Earth attempts to be generously inclusive, stipulated that no children having less than one-fourth Indian blood and no child under the age of six or more than the age of twenty-one could be included under contract without special permission from the Commissioner of Indian Affairs."

Federal schools, and mission schools subsidized by the government, were the magnet institutions of assimilation policies: through the acceptance and denials of certain tribal world views and cultural values, curriculum and instructional manners, the federal blueprints for assimilation became the special burdens of several generations of tribal children.

"With the best of intentions," Sister Carol Berg concludes in her dissertation, "boarding schools across the nation, whether government-run or sectarian, stripped their Indian wards of their native identity. In the name of Christianization and civilization, Indian children were made to wear white people's clothing, speak the English language exclusively, and eat white people's food. The Indian children were caught between two ways of life—one lived within the walls of the boarding school and the other lived primarily in the out-of-doors of the Indian village, albeit only at vacation times. . . ." John Rogers and other students at the mission schools draw most of their stories from their best memories, and transform some adversities into humor, imaginative expressions, woodland dreams, and compassionate trickeries downtown in the new white world.

GEOMETRIC BLOOD AND UNTRIBAL EDUCATION
■

Karl Menninger, psychiatrist and chairman of the board of the Menninger Foundation, testified before the Senate Subcommittee on Indian Education, that children are damaged when their first sources of identities are disrupted, "when you tell him his language is no good, when you tell him that his color is not right or imply it by surrounding him with people of a different color, habits, and status. . . ."

Robert Bergman, psychiatrist and former director of Mental Health Programs of the United States Indian Health Service, writes that "separating Indian children from their parents and tribes has been one of the major aims of governmental Indian services for generations. The assumption is that children and particularly those in any kind of difficulty would be better off being raised by someone other than their own parents."

Lewis Meriam, in his report "The Problem of Indian Administration," which was published in 1928 by the Institute for Government Research, points out that tribal families have been subjected to "peculiar strains growing out of their relation to the government. . . . Insofar as the government has sacrificed real and vital adult education to the formal education of children in institutions it has handicapped a primitive people in their development, and the Indians have little to show to repay them for the sorrows of broken homes.

"The loss of children tends still further to disrupt the family through the loosening of marital ties. Normally husband and wife have a strong bond in their common responsibility for children. To take away this responsibility is to encourage a series of unions with all the bad social consequences that accompany impermanence of marital relations." John Rogers learned that his parents were separated when he returned home from federal boarding school.

Professor Gerasimo at
Wahpeton Indian School,
1969. Photo by the author.

The United States is not the first government in the world to demand so much from racial categories and measurements of blood and
tribal descent, but the practice of determining tribal identities by
geometric degrees of blood, or blood quantums, as if blood could be
measured in degrees, has elevated a racist unscientific method to the
level of a federal statute. On the other hand, the federal government
pursued policies of both elimination and assimilation of tribal cultures,
while on the backhand, mixedbloods were stranded like dandelions between the stumps on new meadows. Some mixedbloods were cast in
literature and official reports as the griseous reminders of the romantic
past, or the loose coins from the economic rape of the land, but whatever
the images, mixedbloods were clearcut, with few exceptions, from the
political present. The exceptions were those mixedbloods who did not
argue for tribal rights. Elected officials expected the tribes to vanish,
which could explain in part the apparent ease with which the federal
government negotiated treaties, certain that in one or two generations
tribal cultures would no longer exist; but tribal populations have increased
in the past century and even more mixedbloods have been elected to
tribal governments on reservations and have assumed leadership positions in urban tribal organizations.

The application of mixedblood geometric scores was not a form of tribal cultural validation. Skin color and blood quantums were not the means the tribe used to determine identities. The Anishinaabeg "classified a person Indian if he lived with them and adopted their habits and mode of life," according to David Beaulieu, former chairman of the Department of American Indian Studies at the University of Minnesota. Some tribal people, he explained at a colloquium on tribal identities, "focus on style of dress as the main feature in distinguishing Indian and mixedblood. Indians wore breachcloth and had braids in their hair whereas mixed-bloods wore hats and pants. . . . Percentage of Indian and white blood was not a determining factor in distinguishing a mixedblood. . . . For the most part the distinction was cultural." These tribal distinctions, which were not racial but experiential, were not adopted by the federal government. Beaulieu pointed out that through treaties the government "attempted to render fixed and static definitions of mixedbloods and Indians not only for the people alive at the moment but to their descendants."

Harold Goodsky, former county probation officer who moved back to the reservation, is a fine teller of stories in the tribal oral tradition. He cuts each verb with care, right at the tense intersections of tribal identities. "I sat at this huge government desk," he said with his face turned toward the sun, " and wrote the word *Indian* over and over again until it seemed to disappear . . . *Indian, Indian, Indian,* and then I asked myself, who, how, what does it mean. . . ?

"I sat there next to my official red telephone writing *Indian, Indian, Indian,* over and over again. I was really befuddled. . . . Who knows what I was thinking about at the time.

"Who am I. . . ?

"Something the white man named and made up in histories and treaties. . . . I was chained in a dream and thought about us all being named by a psychopath like Columbus. . . .

"But I could never be me without my color," he said, holding his hands out and turning them over and over. "I would be nobody without my color. . . . I don't know about the name *Indian* that we all answer to, I don't know that much about history, the history that white men tell, but I know that I have my color."

Goodsky has his color and he speaks the language of the Anishinaabeg, but tribal identities are more complex to him than skin color and a tribal language. He emphasizes in his stories a sense of tribal humor, trust, and a love for people and the land. These attributes in a person are more important, he believes, than the "science fiction degrees of blood."

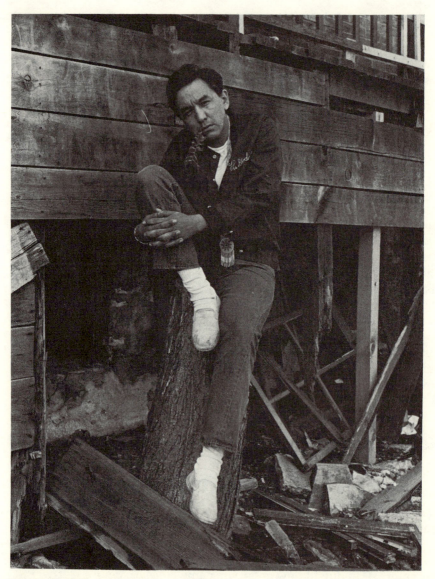

Harold Goodsky, probation
officer, 1967. Photo by the
author.

The students at a small private college were asked to define the word
Indian during a special program on tribal cultures. The following are a
selection of the definitions offered by the students:

Indian is a cultural nationality.

They are a race with a distinct culture.
Real Americans.
Redskins.
A member of the mongolian race.
Indian means friend.
A human being.
Indian is a person.
Indian is an ethnic group.
A wild savage.
Indian means man.

Two students, of about five hundred who responded, defined an Indian as a native of India. Three students were aware that, through a navigational error, thousands of distinct tribal cultures on this continent were homogenized into a single word. The use of the word *Indian* is seldom clear; the word seems to have a different abstract meaning to each reader. Some tribal people become Indians in the word, pantribal, unclear, and separated from distinct traditional cultures. Tribal people must bear special linguistic burdens when the dominant white culture seems to know more about the Indians it invented than anyone.

Anishinaabeg high school students from various reservations were asked to write about what being an Indian means to them. The students were participants in a special leadership training program.

Student from the Nett Lake Reservation

I think the Chippewa Indian is slowly dying. Right now there are plenty of Indians in the United States but very few full-blooded Ojibways. In Minnesota there is a large number of Indians but also the fact that they're of mixed blood. Right now the modern Indian has very many opportunities, the same as a white man. There are some that work their way up to a high position at their place of income and in the community. Yet there are others who don't seem to care. . . .

Student from the Leech Lake Reservation

I think the Indians are great lovers. . . . A lot of Indians have a little French blood in them. The French are supposed to be great lovers. Maybe that is why they are great lovers. And they don't like to be seen making love because they are not as proud as they used to be. . . .

Student from the Fond du Lac Reservation

I think there is a little difference between the Indians and other people. The Indians have a little darker skin and some are smarter than the rest. Some people judge the Indians by their outward appearance. They

Students at Indian Circle,
White Earth Reservation,
1968. Photo by the author.

don't know what's going on inside. The Indians also are very shy, and some talk right out when they are spoken to. Some have a very bad temper; when they are joked around with they get mad and blow up. With others they take it as a joke as it was meant to be. The Indian girls are the love type whenever they see a cute boy. They giggle or try to make a hit. One thing about being an Indian, you have to take things as they come, like when other people talk about you, you just don't blame them because they don't know what they're talking about. . . .

Student from the White Earth Reservation

Almost all of my heritage is European, about one fourth is Indian. Of my four nationalities, French, English, Irish, and Indian, I am most proud of my Indian heritage. There are a lot of Indians I know who are ashamed of their Indian heritage, but if you really stop and think about it, why should they? They probably feel that their ancestors were very barbaric but they were very artistic people. . . .

Ervin Sargent, former director of the Minneapolis Regional Native American Center, said that more people are identifying as Indian because it has become a good thing to be this decade. "In my generation we slumped down in our seats when the word Indian was mentioned. I think in the next generation the young people will be more aware of the angles of identity and the invented things about being Indian in the white society."

Sargent was born at White Earth and attended reservation schools before moving to the city. "The Indians who identify the strongest today are having trouble dealing with their identity when they marry white," he explained, "so they make special rules of identity in their organizations. Some Indians who don't have the pigment are recognized as Indian by their names. . . . But the identity thing is hard to understand. Some white men know more about being Indian than I do, because they have spent a long time talking to the old people. . . ."

Kent Smith was born on the White Earth Reservation and attended public school at Cass Lake on the Leech Lake Reservation. Smith is a sculptor, a graduate in fine arts from the University of Minnesota, and the director of Indian Studies at Bemidji State University. Smith said that in high school he thought of himself as an Indian person only in the sense of cultural and social deprivation. "I haven't been told much about the past. . . . There was very little discussion about Indian culture in our family.

"One day I came home from school and found this Indian outfit on the wall and learned that my father was going to be in a parade," he said, standing by his metal sculpture in his studio. "I was fourteen years old

Students at Indian Circle,
White Earth Reservation,
1968. Photo by the author.

then and I started thinking about my culture. . . . I have never really had
to be an Indian because I wasn't brought up to be an Indian. . . . I was
not brought up with a cultural awareness of the past, partly because I
was never exposed to powwows and Indian social events. . . . Trying
to be an Indian to me now would be the whole thing—the language and
moving back to live on the reservation as an Indian," he said in a gentle
tone of voice.

"Being an Indian is being related to the people," said Lee Cook, who
was born on the Red Lake Reservation and now directs an economic
development program in Minneapolis. "It is the beautiful freedom to go
back to the reservation—to the peace that is really mine." Cook has twice
been an unsuccessful candidate for public office on his home reservation.

FIREWATER LABELS AND METHODOLOGIES

■

*To be human means to stand in
need of solace, of comfort in our
grief or loss or in the painful
throes of anxiety . . . to experience the pain in concert with
our fellows, and to share our
perceptions of meaning, however
fleeting or partial, amidst confusion and despair is to be solaced,
and at a price which, unbearable
as it might seem, saves us from
resigning our powers of decision
to others.*

Norman Jacobsen,
Pride and Solace

■

Plain Johnson, deep in cigarette smoke, hunkers over the wads of paper
labels he peeled from seven bottles of cheap beer at the back of the bar.
From a short distance he seems to be folded in the narrow booth, at the
neck and stomach, a racial monad with swollen fingers. His bare elbows
are thick, burnished from the tilt of his trunk, but there is nothing plain
about this mixedblood tribal man who resisted social conversion in a foster
home and saved his soul from the welfare state. In the afternoon Plain
is a high altitude window washer, at night he drinks beer in a tribal bar,
and in the morning he writes poems and studies literature at a small
private college.

Seventeen years earlier, when he was nine and known as Samuel
American Horse, he was removed, like the tribes from their places on
the earth to reservations, from his mother because she was accused of
being an alcoholic. Samuel and his two sisters were separated and placed
in foster homes for adoption. Samuel assumed a new surname and
deserted the fosterage of seven white families in six years; he resisted
the sentimental gestures of the new welfare missionaries; and he refused

113

to reveal his tribal name in public. Plain declared his foster nickname in a racist culture, a name he claims he will bear until his mother returns and he locates his sisters, an unusual protest.

Plain peels the label on one more bottle.

The United States Corps of Engineers contracted for the construction of the Garrison Dam to hold back the Missouri River in North Dakota. Elbowoods, a small tribal village, the home and birthplace of Marleen American Horse, fell beneath the new flood, the federal creation of Lake Sakakawea, on the Fort Berthold Reservation.

Marleen American Horse came to the cities with a single change of clothes in a brown paper sack and an old reservation allotment map that marked her place on the earth before the flood. Not before the great mythical tribal flood, which balanced the sacred earth, but before the flood of white men and their pleasure boats.

Marleen married a white man after the flood, a truck driver who turned violent toward tribal women when he was drunk, which was three times a week, and he expressed his love for her on the same schedule. Three mixedblood children later, two with dark skin and one with light, and a decade since the flood, she migrated from bar to bar to be with men who abused her for her sins. She became a despondent alcoholic. Drinking was all she could do to ease the guilt and pain from being drunk. She remembered her children, alone at night in a cold apartment. She smiled as best she could with numb lips, and turned under the memories of her sacred tribal past.

Marleen American Horse lost her children to the welfare state. Samuel and his two sisters were removed and placed in foster homes. Now, she was alone with her weakness and guilt. One winter morning when she returned from the bars, walking through the fresh snow to her small apartment, she discovered that she had been evicted. The locks had been changed overnight. An eviction notice was on the door. Her television set, her few clothes, simple memorabilia, a picture of her grandfather at a treaty conference, and the reservation map showing her birthplace, the few material objects remaining in her name, were gone, stolen, or given away. She slumped on the stairs outside the building and began to weep for the loss of the past and her children. She wanted little more than to be loved in a cold and insensitive world.

Plain peels another label.

Tribal friends, and those who witness the attention that writers and social scientists give to his adverse experiences, find humor in the serious presentation of his past. The eagle feather on his black hat and the beaded floral patterns on his wide belt and watchband remind the white world of his pantribal traditions, while his dark skin determines the distance he feels in the dominant culture.

Plain is not detached from his tribal friends at the bar; he is separated from their expectations of his behavior as he had been from the values of the white foster families where he was placed as a child. He holds his birth name back; a secret, he explains, a sacred dream place where he finds his shadow and spiritual center, but he calls out his birth name in public when he is drunk, when he is aggressive and sentimental.

American Horse . . . American Horse, my sacred name is American Horse, he chants as he stumbles through the dark when the bar is closed. In the morning he tells tribal stories in his poems, and then he cleans windows from the outside.

"Over the course of socialization, people learn about drunkenness what their society 'knows' about drunkenness; and, accepting and acting upon the understandings thus imparted to them, they become the living confirmation of their society's teachings," write Craig MacAndrew and Robert Edgerton in *Drunken Comportment.* The authors set aside most common sense arguments about the effects of alcohol on tribal people and conclude "that drunken comportment is an essentially *learned* affair."

Nancy Oestreich Lurie, in her article, "The World's Oldest On-Going Protest Demonstration: North American Drinking Patterns," writes that in her observation, "Indian people are more likely to get drunk when they feel thwarted in achieving Indian rather than white goals. . . . Indian drinking is an established means of asserting and validating Indianness and will be either a managed and culturally patterned recreational activity or else not engaged in at all in direct proportion to the availability of other effective means of validating Indianness."

Mark Lender and James Martin point out in *Drinking in America* that tribal cultures have been the exception to the rules of temperate drinking from the first contact with white colonists. The colonists "remained comfortable about alcohol for themselves," but expressed fear that the use of alcohol by tribal people and blacks "could be dangerous to overall societal stability.

"The colonial view of Indian drinking, that red men could not hold their liquor, was in fact the beginning of a long-standing stereotype of the impact of alcohol on the tribes. Many early settlers believed Indians to be uncivilized—nothing more than 'savages'; therefore, any sign of intemperate behavior served to confirm that image. Some modern anthropologists have termed the so-called Indian drinking problem the 'firewater myth.' This stereotype not only followed the white frontier line," the authors assert, ". . . but in many respects has survived into the present."

Lender and Martin explain that most tribal cultures were "unfamiliar with beverage alcohol before the invasion of the whites. Most tribes got their first taste from the explorers and adventurers who preceded the influx of settlers. . . ." Research has never revealed an unbiased translation of the "firewater myth," nor clinical evidence that tribal people have a genetic weakness or predisposition to alcohol. The authors explain that "some tribes learned to drink from the wrong whites: fur traders, explorers, or fishing crews, all of whom drank hard and, frequently, in a fashion not condoned by the social norms in traditional, settled colonial communities.

"Some whites, for a variety of motives, encouraged binge drinking among the Western Indians," the authors conclude. "Not all tribes succumbed: They either shunned the white man's alcohol or learned to assimilate it without major cultural disruption. But others, like many of the Eastern Indians, fell afoul of fur traders and land speculators who employed established methods of getting Indians drunk before making deals with them. The shrewdest traders refused to negotiate with a sober Indian."

Ray Allen Billington, in *Land of Savagery Land of Promise*, asserts that "few observers were willing to admit that drinking was an escape-hatch from the poverty and humiliation that accompanied the shattering of their culture. . . ." He participates in the complaisant victimization theme that the "true villains were the storekeepers and traders who plied them with liquor to cheat them of their lands and goods."

In response to these preconceptions and fears of white settlers, the federal government enacted legislation purporting to protect tribal cultures from unscrupulous whites. The new laws, however, regulated frontier resources, economies, and territorial settlements. In 1832 the government prohibited liquor in tribal communities. It was not until 1953 that the racist law prohibiting the sale of liquor to tribal people was repealed. The federal response to the excessive consumption of alcohol in white families was much less severe: The Eighteenth Amendment to the Constitution of the United States, or the "Prohibition Amendment," which forbids the manufacture and sale of alcoholic beverages, was ratified in 1920 and repealed thirteen years later.

"Perhaps no stereotype has been so long-lasting and so thoroughly ensconced in our social fabric as that of the 'drunken Indian.' Our federal government," Joseph Westermeyer writes, "gave it official recognition by prohibiting the sale of beverage alcohol to Indian people for over a century. Until recently, many missionary groups required that Indian converts take a pledge of total abstinence." Westermeyer, in his article, " 'The

Drunken Indian': Myths and Realities," examines the common misconceptions which flow from the "nonlogical stereotype" of tribal cultures and beverage alcohol.

"*Indians cannot hold their liquor.* This stereotype presumes that Indian people who do so to excess and inevitably encounter problems as a result of their alcohol usage. Generally this presumed tendency is felt to be due to some inherent racial trait that results in alcohol's affecting Indians in a specific and unusual manner. . . .

"*Alcoholism rates are very high among Indians.* First, we have the problem of what comprises a case of alcoholism. In the opinion of most people, simply imbibing alcohol or behaving in an intoxicated manner is not a sufficient criterion for alcoholism. . . . Considerable differences exist among tribes, even taking into account the small populations of some tribes that make reliable intertribal comparisons difficult. Also, within tribes there are subgroup differences, and within subgroups there are considerable individual differences. These differences, and the reasons for them, have been neglected in most studies," Westermeyer points out in his article. When "Indian rates are compared with national averages, some groups and tribes do have rates of alcohol-related problems that exceed the mean, and some have rates that are much lower. . . .

"*Alcoholism is the major problem among Indian people.* Even among Indian groups that do have high rates of alcohol-related problems, it is difficult to know whether a given problem is caused by alcohol or by various social, economic, historical, cultural, and/or political factors. Alcohol problems are often associated in a given individual with such stresses as migration from the reservation to a non-Indian community; racial and ethnic prejudice; health impairment; unemployment or marginal economic status; outside interference by non-Indian social agencies in family and community affairs; and lack of control in his own community over the education of his children, law enforcement, religious institutions, and health and welfare resources.

"For any one Indian or group of Indians it is difficult to separate racial prejudice, family disintegration, or economic oppression from alcohol in the genesis of various problems. However," Westermeyer emphasizes, "the danger exists that if alcoholism is focused on as the biggest problem, urgent political and economic issues may be ignored. This is especially true because much of what is done regarding alcoholism is done at the individual level, ignoring important social, cultural, and intercultural problems. . . ."

Westermeyer points out that tribal alcohol problems "bear many resemblances to those common to many ethnic groups in the United

States." He concludes that attention to tribal alcoholism "should not mask or preclude attention to the many social problems and inequities against which Indian people now struggle. . . ."

The National Institute of Mental Health has reported that alcohol-related deaths for American Indians are four to five times higher than for the general public. Two-thirds of those deaths are caused by cirrhosis of the liver. Alcohol is also related to higher arrest rates, accidents, homicide, suicide, and spouse and child abuse. In the past decade, there has been a dramatic increase in public funds for research and training and treatment programs in tribal communities for problem drinkers.

The Juel Fairbanks Aftercare Residence, for example, is a treatment center serving alcoholics, most of whom are tribal people, in Ramsey County, Minnesota. Laura Wittstock and Michael Miller, authors of a report on alcoholism based on interviews with tribal people who were treated at the center in Saint Paul, estimate that about half of the tribal population in the nation is chemically dependent. Forty percent more are affected as families and relatives. "Virtually the entire American Indian population is affected, directly or indirectly, by alcoholism," the authors assert in their report, which was published by the Center for Urban and Regional Affairs at the University of Minnesota.

"Problem drinking and alcoholism are most prevalent among those Indian people who are the least acculturated to urban life," the authors point out. Other studies, however, emphasize the opposite view, that acculturation is *not* the most important factor, that deviant behavior is *not* explained by acculturation.

Plain Johnson seldom drinks alone; he hunkers in a booth at the back of the bar, deep in smoke, with his tribal friends, the friends who understand his gestures and who give meaning to his experiences at the cold intersections in the cities. Plain counts all his tribal friends as his brothers.

Samuel leans back in the booth with a wide smile, a simple pose he likes to strike at least once a night. He drinks gallons of cheap beer and tells trickster stories in the best oral tradition; he is a fine teacher in a small college, and he is a problem drinker.

Cecelia drinks vodka and fruit juices and bears a perpetual cigarette with a short curved ash as she fingers the ends of her tangled black hair. She is a tribal mixedblood, the mother of four children who have been placed in foster care homes because she is an alcoholic. She is at home in the back of the bar with her friends.

Ramon is a medical doctor, the first in his tribe to earn the high honor of becoming a biomedical healer; and he is an alcoholic. He practices medicine on the road, at tribal social and cultural events, and at the back of tribal bars in the cities. This morning he was invited to meet with tribal students at a small college, summoned as a model of tribal achievements, but when he stumbled out of the elevator with his trousers unzipped, and vomit stains on his shirt, the event was cancelled.

Harmon has been on the bottle since he lost his right arm in combat. He can trace his descent to a circle of proud warriors. Each morning he begins his series of toasts to his phantom arm, his three wives, and the children he seldom visits.

Charles was never employed for more than one month at one place because work interfered with his drinking. The old mixedblood trapper was a modern tribal nomad, a severe alcoholic who moved back to the reservation and froze to death three feet from the door of his cabin in a snow storm. Plain Johnson, and all his friends from the tribal bar, remembered the trapper at a traditional wake and tribal burial.

Tribal cultures are burdened with statistical summaries, romantic preoccupations, cultural inventions, social expectations, adverse public attitudes, in both tribal and urban white worlds. The view that tribal people have a predisposition or genetic weakness to alcohol is a racist response to a serious national problem. The notion that tribal people drink to relume their past memories as warriors will neither explain nor mend the broken figures who blunder drunk and backslide through cigarette smoke from one generation to the next. Separations from tribal traditions through marriage or acculturation do not explain the behavior associated with drunkenness. Tribal cultures are diverse and those individuals who are studied at the bar, or on the streets, are unique, alive, and troubled, not static entities from museums or the notebooks of culture cultists. There is some humor over the adversities tribal people bear in racist societies, but there is not much to laugh about in the families of alcoholics.

"Outside of residence in a concentration camp," writes George Vaillant, in *The Natural History of Alcoholism*, "there are very few sustained human experiences that make one the recipient of as much sadism as does being a close family member of an alcoholic."

Two common themes are evident in most of the studies of tribal drinking, according to Michael Everett, an editor of *Drinking Behavior Among Southwestern Indians*. The first theme is that tribal drinking is somehow different from other drinking, and the second theme is that tribal drinking, in spite of the problems and abuses of alcohol, "has a number of positive aspects that are often ignored or denied."

Edwin Lemert, for example, studied cultures on the northwest coast and emphasized the positive use of alcohol in the revival of traditional patterns of tribal leadership and ritual when traditional behavior was denied by the white dominant culture. Other studies conclude that tribal drunkenness is a *positive* approach to social integration, a method of survival under cultural duress and the stress of acculturation in the white world.

Jerrold Levy and Stephen Kunitz, in their research on tribal drinking in the southwest, questioned whether tribal drinking is a "retreatist or escapist response to social disintegration," or whether the behavior is compatible with "tribal institutional values." The authors conclude that deviant behavior associated with alcohol can be explained in terms of social type, and that the "persistence of patterns of suicide and homicide over long periods indicates that neither increased acculturation nor increased alcohol use have been the major factors influencing these types of social deviance. . . ."

Thomas Hill, who studied tribal drinking in Sioux City, Iowa, writes in his dissertation, " 'Feeling Good' and 'Getting High': Alcohol Use of Urban Indians," that "multiple sets of drinking norms or standards exist within the Indian population. . . ." He points out that what is acceptable or unacceptable consumption of alcohol depends "upon whose perception we adopt. . . . I have tried to show that at any single point in time many factors may play a role in 'causing' an individual to engage in excessive or problem drinking: social pressure, few social controls limiting drinking, various psychological motives, and biochemical and physiological variables." The tribal people he studied "were not suffering from a massive state of 'deculturation' or sociocultural disorganization. . . ."

American Indians resist the traditional methods of treating alcoholism, assert Laura Wittstock and Michael Miller in their report. "For many Indians, drinking is such a central element in social life that to avoid it means to reject friends, relatives," and familiar social places. "The solution to alcoholism has as much to do with improving the conditions of life for Indians as it does with improving treatment programs," the authors explain. "A major difficulty for many Indians in remaining sober is finding an environment of friends and a social life that is free of alcohol. There is a constant pressure to be in social and family situations where alcohol is present." The authors point out that their research "uncovered fewer persons raised by foster parents, particularly white foster parents, than was expected. Studies from other areas have indicated that as many as twenty-five to thirty percent of those surveyed were raised by white foster parents and their alcoholism rates were higher than the general Indian population."

Wittstock and Miller conclude that "alcoholism is but one symptom of the economic and social conditions faced by the Indians. Key among these conditions is unequal access to the economic benefits of society."

The problems of alcoholism in tribal communities are as burdensome as some of the theories and proposed solutions. Even to the biased outsider the definitions of tribal alcoholism, and the explanations of drunken behavior, seldom lead to common treatment methods or reliable prevention plans. The diverse experiences of tribal people decamp from simple racial solutions to the problem. Histories tumble with each drink; tribal memories and colonial theories break from the masculine pleasures stored in national advertisements for the beverage alcohol.

Levy and Kunitz, for example, contend that "the pattern of alcohol use differs depending on degree of acculturation. . . . To be like a white man means, in part, drinking like one."

Ron Wood, a Navajo who works in a public health program, expresses a similar view, that the "more acculturated a Native American person is, the more his drinking pattern tends to resemble the Anglo pattern of drinking." He points out how drinking habits differ from tribe to tribe. "The Navajo drinking pattern is generally of an open, boisterous manner with friends, while the Hopi pattern is generally of a singular, secretive, or less boisterous nature. To be effective, a Native American alcoholism counselor must be aware of these differences among individual clients."

Research seldom focuses on the "practical issues of treatment," or the prevention of alcohol problems, according to Michael Everett, editor of *Drinking Behavior Among Southwestern Indians*, because the studies emphasize the "positive functions of drinking and drunkenness." Everett contends that theories and research methodologies have contributed little to the meanings of tribal drinking practices, "and even less to the development of effective treatment and prevention strategies for Indian alcoholism and problem drinking."

Thomas Hill, an anthropologist, did not consider treatment programs in his studies of tribal drinking in Sioux City, but he concludes, nevertheless, that "a program which attempts to utilize a single treatment approach will be inadequate. . . ."

Wittstock and Miller, however, include treatment strategies in their research and report. Deriving their information from interviews, the authors are critical of confrontation therapies, those which challenge the behavior of alcoholics, because when these therapies are used by white counselors, the tribal clients could perceive the methods "as symbolic of the conflict between white and Indian cultures." The authors conclude that "better treatment programs" should emphasize the need for "Indian staff and counselors, and making use of Indian culture and spiritual values in the course of treatment."

Certain traditional tribal spiritual practices, such as herbal or symbolic healing, are culture specific, limited to one cultural experience. Other religious and spiritual events, such as the sacramental use of peyote, have been successful in the treatment of alcohol problems. The Native American Church, which uses peyote in ceremonies, and other pantribal fundamentalist movements, have been effective rehabilitation experiences for some tribal people.

These are positive methods of treatment and rehabilitation, but punitive approaches to the problem also are taken that prohibit the use of alcohol. There seems to be less tolerance of drunkenness at social and tribal spiritual events; signs prohibiting the use of alcohol or drugs appear more often on the doors of tribal centers.

Plain Johnson, and other tribal people at the bar, are marginal consumers of alcohol in the annals of advertisers. Tribal consumption, however, does have some commercial value. Some owners will sponsor social and athletic events for their tribal customers, but most owners of tribal drinking places encourage the consumption of alcohol for personal profits. The federal government collects revenue from the sale of beverage alcohol; the funds that are returned to tribal communities are used to establish new treatment bureaucracies that focus on individuals rather than on larger social problems.

Being Indian, Ron Wood points out, "is not enough qualification to be a successful counselor, nor is the fact that a person is a recovered alcoholic sufficient qualification. . . . A certain amount of technical training is necessary to be a good counselor, but the most important criterion is having a good heart and empathy to help fellow" tribal people.

Meanwhile, back at the bar, in the neon light and cigarette smoke, Samuel tells fine trickster stories; Cecelia weeps for the loss of her children when she is sober and curses the welfare workers when she is drunk; Ramon is a radical critic of the medical profession; Harmon has seen too much evil to hide in a fair world; Charles lived in silence most of the time, and though he was not unkind to people or animals, the mongrels on the reservation seemed to shun the old trapper when he stumbled through the woods.

Theoretical definitions and statistical silhouettes are interesting, even useful in raising funds for treatment programs, but the tribal people at the bar are inclined to answer the latest theories that rationalize their behavior with guilt, humor, or derision.

George Vaillant writes that alcoholism reflects "deviant behavior that can be often better classified by sociologists than by physiologists; alcoholism is often better treated by psychologists skilled in behavior therapy than by physicians with all their medical armamentarium. But unlike giving up gambling or fingernail biting, giving up alcohol abuse often requires skilled medical attention during the period of acute withdrawal. Unlike gamblers and fingernail biters, most alcoholics as a result of their disorder develop secondary symptoms that do require medical care. . . ."

Reviewing the treatments and definitions of alcoholism, Vaillant, a psychiatrist at the Harvard Medical School, argues that "calling alcoholism a disease, rather than a behavior disorder, is a useful device both to persuade the alcoholic to admit his alcoholism and to provide a ticket for admission into a health care system."

Vaillant has not studied alcoholism in tribal communities, but in general he points out that alcoholism affects one-third of all American families, and the mortality rate for alcoholics is higher, four times the average. The cost of alcoholism, in lost wages and treatment, is fifty billion dollars a year. In the past decade, according to the author, the federal government has invested one hundred million dollars on alcoholism treatment programs.

Plain peels the last label for the night.

DENNIS OF WOUNDED KNEE

■

Prophets are seldom honored among a people who feel that they are masters of their own destiny. A social atmosphere which stimulates a spirit of self-confidence is not one to encourage reliance upon superhuman forces. It is only when the shocks and perils of existence are overwhelming that the individual feels the need for something to support his mortal weakness.

Homer Barnett,
Indian Shakers

■

FEBRUARY 12, 1974
■

Dennis Banks was dressed in secular vestments. He wore beads, bones, leathers, ribbons, and a cultural frown, for his appearance in court, where he was on trial for alleged violations of federal laws in connection with the occupation of Wounded Knee on the Pine Ridge Reservation in South Dakota.

Banks seldom smiles in public. He looked down that afternoon as he stood alone before twelve federal jurors. His focus seemed to shift from table to chair, past the rims and rails in the courtroom, and then he raised his head and told the jurors in his opening statement that he was at Wounded Knee, as charged, and that he was "guilty of asking that the Senate investigate all the conditions that the federal government has imposed upon our people. . . ."

Banks, who is a mixedblood Anishinaabe from the Leech Lake Reservation in Minnesota, and one of the founders of the American Indian Movement, was on trial with Russell Means from the Pine Ridge Reservation.

124

Dennis Banks, 1968. Photo
by the author.

Means, who seems to move in mythic time, overbearing at the brink
of ritualism, thrust his chest forward that morning in court and explained
to the jurors that he would produce evidence to show how the "United
States of America has set up a public tribal government under the foam
and the heel of the Interior Department and the Bureau of Indian Affairs,
but before we get into some of the more specific evidence that we will
introduce, one has to understand what the Indian psyche is all about,
that we have a completely different value system than that of the larger
society. . . . We will introduce evidence of how we've had to go
underground in order to maintain our traditional religion, our traditional
philosophy. . . .

"The Oglala people themselves will be the ones testifying. The Oglala,
some of them will need interpreters, some of them won't be able to speak
very good English, and they will all be scared. . . . We will prove that
at the direction of our traditional chiefs and headmen, just as the treaty
provides, at their direction and with their support, we were directed into Wounded Knee. . . .

"First of all, we believe that all living things come from our sacred
mother earth, all living things, the green things, the winged things of
the air, the four leggeds, the things that crawl and swim and, of course,
the two leggeds. . . . But the important thing in our philosophy is that

we believe we're the weakest things on earth, that the two legged is the weakest thing on earth because we have no direction. . . .

"Now, because we are the weakest things on earth, we do not have a license to exploit or manipulate our brothers and sisters and we also know, because of our role in life, that the buffalo and all other relatives of ours teach us, and so we built our civilization. . . .

"Of course, there is another way. That is to grab the bottle, drink it, go down to the other bar and fight your brothers and sisters just to say, 'Look, I'm a man,' or take the bottle again and go home and mistreat your wife and tell her, 'Look, I'm a man.'

"And there is another way, the way that we will prove that the United States of America, in its genocidal policies against Indian people, forced us to be red-white people. That is the other way, is to cut our hair, put on the ties and become facsimiles of the white man. . . .

"There has been . . . a new way to express our manhood, and that's been the American Indian Movement to express our Indianness. . . . I was an accountant by trade in Cleveland, Ohio, and in the Dakota way, if you cut your hair, that means you're in mourning. And it is our contention that a lot of Dakotas now who are misguided cut their hair because they're mourning because they lost their Indianness.

"Also, when I had my hair cut," Russell Means told the jurors, "I was mistaken for a Chicano, for an Arab, a Hawaiian, a Pakistanian, everything but an American Indian. I'm very proud to be Dakota, and when I walk down the street, I want people to know I'm Indian. . . ."

Dennis Banks told the federal jurors that he was a member of the traditional Oglala Sioux Sun Dance religion, which, he explained in a gentle voice, is a "very sacred religious event where men warriors offer themselves to the great spirit to seek a vision, that we have to go through it for four years and somewhere through those four years we will find that vision; that there must be fasting, that we must give up water, and that we must prove to Mother Earth and all the female objects of this planet, to all the female things, that we would like to share some of the pain. The men warriors would like to share some of the pain that our mothers, that our mothers had, when we were born."

The Sun Dance is a ceremony in which vows are made in sacred preparation for a personal vision. Some participants in the ritual puncture the skin on their chest with wooden skewers which are tied to a sacred tree. Those who seek a vision dance in the circle of the sun until the skewers are torn from their flesh.

"The piercing of the skin," Banks told the jurors that afternoon in federal court, "is a reminder to me that I truly owe myself to Mother Earth and to all the female things of this planet. The most sacred of all Oglala

Dennis Banks and Kahn-
Tineta at a tribal dance,
1968. Photo by the author.

events is the Oglala Sun Dance; and when the flesh was torn from me
I suddenly realized what a great sin, what a great injustice it would be
to lose the Oglala Sioux religion."

Banks seems to represent the dominant male view in his references
to women as "objects" and "things," while at the same time he presents
himself as a tribal traditionalist and a man of peace and spiritual visions.

Banks told the federal jurors that he was called to a meeting on Monday, February 27, 1972, at Calico Hall on the Pine Ridge Reservation. "I
attended this meeting, and the evidence will show that those who were
in attendance at that meeting were Oglala Sioux chiefs, traditional
headmen, medicine men and councilmen. . . .

"I heard an Oglala Sioux woman, two women, address their chiefs
and headmen in their own language. . . . The plea that they made to the
American Indian Movement, two women who were truly the real warriors of Indian society, who saw their own sons dying on the reservations, who saw their own children dying on the way to the hospital. . . .
They asked the medicine men and the headmen, they asked them, where
were the spirits of so long ago that made this nation great, where was
that Indian spirit that the Oglala Sioux nation so many years ago stood
up against the United States Army, and these two women demanded

an answer from the chiefs and those of us who were present, demanded
to know if there were any Indians left in this country, if there were any
Indians left in the United States, Indians who were descendants of those
great Indian heroes of long ago. . . ."

Banks was not seen at Calico Hall on the Pine Ridge Reservation
where five traditional leaders and more than a hundred other tribal people had gathered to consider a scheme to seize Wounded Knee village.
Russell Means was at the meeting, but Banks was at Cherry Creek on
the Cheyenne River Reservation with a television news reporter. Banks
was chauffeured to Wounded Knee by the reporter, but she departed
when federal marshalls surrounded the area.

Monday evening, February 27, 1973, Means was perched on a platform behind a large table at the end of Calico Hall. Lower, in front of
him, the five traditional, or hereditary, leaders were seated in a row on
benches. Means, who did not speak a tribal language then, spoke to the
leaders through Leonard Crow Dog, an interpreter. The traditional leaders
listened to radical entreaties in translation and then retired to the basement of the small building to consider their approval of a plan to seize
Wounded Knee. The leaders conferred for two hours, but postponed their
decision until a second meeting could be held with elected reservation
officials. Means was not pleased with their indecision, as he had expected
the support of the hereditary leaders; he told them not to overlook his
response to their needs on the reservation. We have been invited here,
but remember, he admonished the leaders through a translator, we can
leave to help people in other places.

Banks has denied the mortal limits of his time on the earth; his radical
visage will endure; he will be remembered in cold footnotes and in
humorous stories. Seven years before Wounded Knee, Banks had short
hair and wore a dark suit and narrow necktie. He had been paroled from
prison and posed in conservative clothes then; he did not braid his hair
or express his aspirations to become an urban tribal radical until he and
others realized that the church and state would subsidize protest organizations. It seems ironic now that Banks once opposed the first protest of the
area office of the Bureau of Indian Affairs in Minneapolis. "Demonstrations are not the Indian way," he said then as he wagged his finger at the
director of the American Indian Employment Center, who had organized
the protest to demand equal federal services for urban tribal people.

The American Indian Movement is a radical urban organization whose
members have tried from time to time to return to the reservations as
the warrior heroes of tribal people. To some, the radicals are the heroes
of dominant histories, but to others the leaders of the movement are the
freebooters of racism. The leaders have been paid well for their activities.

American Indian Movement,
Bureau of Indian Affairs,
Minneapolis, 1968. Photo by
the author.

The American Indian Movement was founded in a storefront in Minneapolis about five years before the occupation of Wounded Knee. Banks,
Clyde Bellecourt, Harold Goodsky, George Mitchell, and others organized
a patrol to monitor the activities of police officers in urban tribal communities. The police watch program grew from a membership of foot
soldiers to expensive mobile radio units. The serious issue was police
harassment, but the method of trailing police cars in expensive conver-
tibles became an extravagant satire. The rhetoric was colonial oppression,
the press coverage was excellent then, and thousands of dollars of guilt
money rolled in from church groups, but the organizers of the movement
argued about philosophies and ideologies. Mitchell, an intense in-
dividualist, was dedicated to service in urban communities, whereas
Goodsky worked in corrections before returning to the reservation.

Banks and several others remained in the organization to continue
the confrontation politics with the intellectual and legal assistance of
dozens of romantic white radicals and liberals from the peace movement.
Those tribal people who followed the ideologies of confrontation were
in conflict at times with those who believed that negotiations lead to institutional changes. These differences in ideologies and radical practices
were emphasized in media coverage. News reports created the heroes
of confrontation for an imaginative white audience, but those dedicated

to negotiations were ignored. Reporters have their own professional needs to discover and present adventurous characters and events. Banks and other radical leaders have become the warriors of headlines, but not the heart of the best stories that turn the remembered tribal world.

The political ideologies of the radical tribal leaders are reactions to racism and cultural adversities; that much all tribal people have in common; but the radical rhetoric of the leaders was not learned from traditional tribal people on reservations or in tribal communities. Some of the militant leaders were radicalized in prison, where they found white inmates eager to listen. The poses of tribal radicals seem to mimic the romantic pictorial images in old photographs taken by Edward Curtis for a white audience. The radicals never seem to smile, an incautious throwback to the stoical tribal visage of slower camera shutters and film speeds. The new radicals frown, even grimace at cameras, and claim the atrocities endured by all tribal cultures in first person pronouns.

Some militants decorate themselves in pastiche pantribal vestments, pose at times as traditionalists, and speak a language of confrontation and urban politics. The radical figures were not elected to speak for tribal reservation people, nor were they appointed to represent the interests and political views of elected tribal officials. In response to this criticism, several tribal radicals returned to reservations. Vernon Bellecourt, for example, a member of the American Indian Movement, returned to the White Earth Reservation where he was elected a representative. Bellecourt was an ambitious reservation politician, no less outspoken than he had been in urban tribal politics, and he served his constituents with distinction.

Banks, however, has never faced tribal constituencies in a legitimate election. His influence is media borne; he has carried numerous administrative titles in the past, but his power seems to be ideological, material, and institutional. His most recent academic position, for example, was as chancellor of Daganawidah-Quetzalcoatl University located near Davis, California, where he lived for several years. Banks had become a civil hero in exile, a new banished word warrior, when Governor Jerry Brown denied his extradition to South Dakota, where he had been convicted of riot and assault charges and was wanted on a fugitive warrant.

LEECH LAKE RESERVATION
■

Nine months before the occupation of Wounded Knee, several hundred members of the American Indian Movement carried weapons for the first time, in preparation for an armed confrontation with white people on the opening day of fishing on the Leech Lake Reservation in Minnesota. The militants were prepared and determined to battle for tribal control of hunting and fishing rights on the reservation, rights that had been won in federal court. Their threats were not needed.

Dennis Banks and a dozen armed leaders were invited to a meeting in a tribal center on the first day they arrived on the reservation. The militants marched into a classroom where the meeting was scheduled and sat on little chairs, their knees tucked under their chins. Banks remained in motion, with one hand at his neck in serious thought. He was dressed in hunks of fur, his mountain man outfit that spring.

Simon Howard, then president of the Minnesota Chippewa Tribe, entered the classroom last. He sat on a little chair at the head of the circle and twirled his thumbs over his stomach and considered the arguments between the militants about their places in the radical chain of command. Howard wore a bowling jacket and a floral print porkpie fishing hat, cocked back on his head, in contrast to the new pantribal vestments worn by the militants. Howard was born on the reservation; he had lived there all his life. He called the meeting as an elected reservation official to maintain peace between white people and the urban tribal militants, a proper start with the militants in little chairs.

"All right boys, quiet down now and take your seats again," said Howard. "Now; I don't know everyone here, so let's go around the room and introduce ourselves. . . . Let's start with you over there, stand up and introduce yourself."

The man pushed his feet forward, swung his rifle around, and stood in front of his little chair. "My name is Delano Western, and I'm from Kansas," he said in a trembling voice as he leaned forward and looked down toward the floor. He was dressed in a wide black hat with an imitation silver headband, dark green sunglasses with round lenses, a sweatshirt with "Indian Power" printed on the front, two bandoliers of heavy ammunition, none of which matched the bore of his rifle, a black leather jacket, and a large military bayonet strapped to his waist next to his revolver.

"We came here to die," he said and sat down.

"The white man has stolen our sacred land and violated our treaties time and time again. . . ." Banks said as he paced outside the circle of little chairs.

"Banks, this is a reservation, not a church basement," said a visitor, "save your speech for the white people out back with the cash."

The militants had been invited to live at a church camp that was located on the reservation. The land had been given to the church by the federal government to encourage the establishment of missions and schools to "civilize" the tribes. Several hundred militants lived there for about a week.

The militants had demanded money from white public officials in the area, and when officials refused, radical leaders held a press conference on a rifle range to scare the public.

Banks, dressed in a black velvet shirt, posed for television cameras with LaDonna Harris, wife of Senator Fred Harris from Oklahoma, before he attempted to fire his short-barrel shotgun, which was looped to his waist with rope. As the cameras recorded the event, Banks faced the food cans placed at a distance on the target range, dropped to one knee and drew his shotgun, but the trigger housing caught in the rope holster. Banks stood and tried to draw again, but it stuck a second time. While he untied the rope, the television focused on Russell Means who was firing what he called his "white people shooter," a small-caliber pistol.

The confrontations at the Leech Lake Reservation, unlike those confrontations which followed on other reservations, were, for the most part, little more than verbal battles. Several shots were exchanged one night near the church camp, but no one was injured. An investigation of the incident revealed that several militants had decided to shine for deer that night; seeing what they thought were the eyes of a deer, they opened fire. The animal in the dark was a cow owned by a local farmer, who fired back at the militants. The cow, the militants, and the farmer were unharmed.

Simon Howard, David Munnell, and other elected reservation officials, attorney Kent Tupper, and officials from the United States Department of Justice were responsible for a peaceful resolution of potential armed violence in the area. Tensions were high in the militant church camp, even higher, perhaps, in white communities around the reservation.

"We must go on living on this reservation after you leave," Howard told the militants at their last meeting.

"We are making changes in the courts, not by violence," said Munnell. "We are building for ourselves an economic system and we will continue to fight in the courts for our rights."

Tupper, who represented the Leech Lake Reservation in federal court, told the militants several times during the week that the rights of tribal people must be won according to the law and not by violence.

Some local satirists, however, attributed the mellow verbal confrontation to the weather. The cold rain, some resolved, was all that could distract the urban tribal militants, armed for the first time with new rifles and pistols. Myles Olson, a Minnesota Highway Patrolman for the area, explained that "two days of rain was worth two slop buckets of mace."

WASHINGTON TO WOUNDED KNEE
■

Six months later, Dennis Banks and the American Indian Movement mustered the Trail of Broken Treaties, which earned broad support from urban tribal communities and from church bodies and white liberal organizations. The favors of vicarious constituencies held when the new tribal militants seized the national offices of the Bureau of Indian Affairs, but enthusiasm eroded when it was revealed that the radicals had caused two million dollars in senseless damage to the building and that the leaders had accepted more than sixty thousand dollars in cash to leave town.

Three months later, the militants gathered in Custer, and Rapid City, South Dakota, for a few weeks before their assault on Wounded Knee.

The leaders of the American Indian Movement, with the exception of Dennis Banks on this occasion, were registered at a comfortable downtown motel in Rapid City while their followers, many of whom were on probation and parole and truant from public schools, were stuck at the Mother Butler Center with no food or funds. Local merchants reached an informal agreement that it was better to tolerate shoplifting than to detain the militants and risk possible personal harm and property damage. The leaders, meanwhile, were evicted from the motel when they refused to pay more than two thousand dollars in room and restaurant charges.

"I think you have a good message for this country," said Mayor Donald Barnett when he first met the radical tribal leaders. Later, however, when he had read their criminal records and discovered that they were armed and unwilling to cover their debts, he changed his verbs and metaphors. "People working for civil rights do not carry guns. I have seen the records of these men and you can't sit and negotiate with a man who has a gun. . . . Are these men serious civil rights workers, or are they a bunch of bandits?"

John Peterson, an investigative reporter for the *Detroit News*, writes that the occupation of Wounded Knee "has been financed almost exclusively by federal money." In an article dated March 25, 1973, he quotes a federal official who said that the "Justice Department was all set to move in and make arrests" at Wounded Knee, but when American Indian Movement leaders "threatened to call a press conference and disclose exactly how much financing" they had received from the federal government, the "Justice Department backed off and tried to play for a standoff," hoping the militants would "tire and leave voluntarily." American Indian Movement leaders "have just dusted off and updated the old militant tactic of intimidating government officials until they come through with grants. . . ." Peterson points out that during the year before the occupation of Wounded Knee the American Indian Movement had received about three hundred thousand dollars from the federal government for various programs.

The *Omaha World-Herald*, in an article published March 14, 1973, revealed that three national church organizations had contributed close to three hundred thousand dollars to the American Indian Movement, in addition to the federal funds.

THE INFORMER WAS A PILOT
■

Douglass Durham, an informer for the Federal Bureau of Investigation, and at the same time an advisor to Dennis Banks, reported that in the two years following the occupation of Wounded Knee, the American Indian Movement received more than one million dollars in contributions from various public and private sources. Columbia Studios, for example, paid Banks twenty-five thousand dollars for his consultation on a script about Wounded Knee. The actor Marlon Brando contributed cash, real estate, and properties to the militant leaders.

The Wounded Knee Legal Defense-Offense Committee circulated hundreds of letters to raise funds. "In the interest of justice, and in the belief that everyone is entitled to a fair trial," one letter explained, "we are asking you to contribute. . . ."

United States District Judge Fred Nichol considered the financial condition of Russell Means and Dennis Banks, and ruled that the court appoint two attorneys for each defendant and pay incidental expenses including travel, parking fees, and living expenses during the Wounded Knee trial in Saint Paul.

Leonard Cavise, an attorney responsible for the financial accounting of contributions and expenditures of the legal committee, stated in an affidavit to the court that as of January 8, 1974, the committee had a balance of $316.99 in a checking account at the National Bank of South Dakota in Sioux Falls. Cavise explained that "no religious organization, church or social-welfare group has contributed any funds to the committee for anything other than bail-bond purposes."

Those who believe that the American Indian Movement is a new tribal spiritual movement could be disillusioned by some information critical of the radical leaders and their activities. In a report published and distributed by the militants, the American Indian Movement is defined as "first a spiritual movement, a religious rebirth, and then a rebirth of Indian dignity . . . attempting to connect the realities of the past with the promises of tomorrow." However, in other documents, identified as confidential by the militants, the future policies of the American Indian Movement did not include references to religion or spiritual movements. The American Indian Movement "should prepare a manifesto on the goals and political thought which constitutes the movement," the document reveals. The movement will also "formulate an international coordination with world powers . . . create a Latin American liberation organization . . . establish working contracts with all liberation fronts in South America . . . establish a political action committee to fully exploit the democratic American system as long as it exists to utilize the system for Indian gains . . . create an action arm to unify all resistance groups operating in the United States so as to form a functioning coalition with all . . . create a labor relations committee . . . prepare a detailed plan for the abolition" of Bureau of Indian Affairs control over one "major reservation and fight for this freedom through the courts. . . ." Other documents explain that the "natural evolution" of the American Indian Movement "will result in the establishment of Indian member states based on tribal boundaries. These member states could form a coalition or a congress of Indian peoples. Reservations are the natural beginning of state formations." These ideas were imposed, not elected by tribal people.

During the summer, following the occupation of Wounded Knee on the Pine Ridge Reservation, Dennis Banks drove to Yellowknife on Great Slave Lake in Northwest Territories. There, to avoid possible arrest, Banks lived with the director of the Native Indian Brotherhood of Canada, according to information provided by Douglass Durham at a senate hearing before the Subcommittee to Investigate the Administration of the Internal Security Act, of the Committee of the Judiciary. Senator James Eastland, chairman of the subcommittee, called but one witness on April 6, 1976. The purpose of the hearing, the chairman explained, was "to try to establish whether there is, in fact, reason for believing that the American Indian Movement is a radical subversive organization rather than an organization committed to improving the lot of the American Indians." Basing its opinion on the testimony of Durham, and on various documents and reports, the subcommittee, in a report published in September 1976, concluded that "The American Indian Movement does not speak for the American Indians. . . . It is a frankly revolutionary organization which is committed to violence, calls for the arming of American Indians, has cached explosives and illegally purchased arms, plans kidnappings. . . . It has many foreign ties, direct and indirect—with Castro's Cuba, with China . . . with the Palestine Liberation Organization," and with the Irish Republican Army. The subcommittee also found that the American Indian Movement has "maintained contact with and has received propaganda and other support from a large number of left extremist organizations,

including the Weather Underground, the Communist Party, the Trot-
skyists, the Symbionese Liberation Army, the Black Panther Party," and
other radical organizations in the United States.

Douglass Frank Durham was the national security director of the
American Indian Movement when he was exposed as an informer for the
Federal Bureau of Investigation. He was a former patrolman with the Des
Moines, Iowa, police department; in March 1973, he traveled to Wound-
ed Knee as a photographer for the newspaper *Pax Today*. Six months later,
he had assisted Dennis Banks in his one month escape to the wilderness.
Durham pretended that he was a tribal mixedblood from the Lac Courte
Oreille Reservation in Wisconsin.

Banks was free on bond for his involvement in the occupation of
Wounded Knee when he was indicted by a grand jury for his participation in a riot at Custer, South Dakota, six months earlier. Durham told
the subcommittee that Banks instructed him, while he was at Yellowknife,
to establish and maintain a "railroad" for tribal militants, "a means
whereby you can move people, warriors, weapons," in overnight accom-
modations between states. Banks promoted Durham to his personal
security director and pilot for the American Indian Movement. The informer testified that he was the only person who knew that Banks had
moved from Yellowknife to Rae Lakes, a remote island in Northwest Territories near the Arctic Circle. He hid there with several friends for about
one month while Durham raised money for his second bond.

Durham told the subcommittee that Banks assumed the name Sherman Eagle and was given false identification to return to the United States.
Durham, a licensed pilot, rented a small airplane for the return trip. Banks,
who was wanted on a fugitive warrant, was concerned, even with false
identification, that he would be arrested at the international border.
Durham testified that "he was concerned about radar and other devices
picking us up because he felt they were on our trail. So, we flew below
the systems through inclement weather, and sometimes through canyons,
at a couple hundred miles an hour, and did make it back into a small
abandoned field out at the edge of town, where we landed. We sneaked
Dennis Banks into Rapid City and into the courtroom," where he posted
his bond before he was arrested.

Durham further testified that "George Roberts advocated spiriting
Dennis Banks to Cuba, and in my presence called Dr. Faustino Perez,
in New Mexico, to establish contact with Fidel Castro. Perez was an old
friend of Ahmed Ben Bella from Algeria, and was quite involved in the
landing in Cuba."

"The Bay of Pigs?" asked the subcommittee counsel.

"No; when Castro first obtained power in Cuba," Durham responded.

"All right, when he came out of the mountains."

"Right, out of the mountains," Durham continued. "Dr. Fausto—as he is referred to—advised Roberts that he would have the information sent in a diplomatic pouch to Cuba and at that point Roberts," who was from Venice, California, and the owner of the Inca Manufacturing Company, "advised his wife to travel to Mexico City to meet Faustino Perez, who was supposedly, or allegedly, a friend of hers. Anyway, she returned with the information that Castro had rejected the plan because he felt that there would be increasing relations with the United States. . . ."

"He was expecting this to disturb the increasingly better relations with the United States?" the subcommittee counsel asked the witness.

"That's correct, sir," Durham responded to the counsel who asked most of the questions at the hearing. "A suggestion was issued, allegedly from Dr. Faustino Perez, that Banks should approach the People's Republic of China for a move in the direction they would indicate, which would later allow him to go to Latin America and become the new Che Guevara because he was a Native American person."

"Was all this arrangement in contemplation that he would be found guilty at the trial?" asked the subcommittee counsel.

"In contemplation not of his being found guilty at the trial," the witness explained, "but rather being seized at the end of the trial by the Custer County authorities and jailed until they held a trial for him. It was later decided that we would return and if Dennis Banks were to be found either guilty or not guilty, if there was a motion by Custer County authorities in South Dakota to arrest him, he would make a stand at Rosebud. Groups of Indians around the country started gathering arms and moving toward Rosebud, South Dakota. . . ."

SANCTUARIES FROM VENGEANCE

■

"Judge Nichol dismissed the charges, and the attorneys, William Kunstler, and Mark Lane, specifically Mark Lane, started a 'jurors and others for reconciliation movement' where he got the jurors and others to write letters. . . ." Dennis Banks did not make his last stand at Rosebud, however. He moved to California where, Durham testified, "we were brought out at the expense of Columbia Studios, put up at the Hilton Hotel . . . limousine service and chateaubriand dinners, and were just the victims of 'horrifying oppression' for quite some time there. I might add that during all this time, though, Banks was still drawing three hundred dollars a month in food stamps. . . ."

The Federal Bureau of Investigation, acting on a warrant from South Dakota, arrested Banks near San Francisco where he had been in hiding for several months. Marlon Brando, Jane Fonda, and others, publicized his cause; a petition, signed by more than a million citizens, supported Dennis Banks. The Attorney General of South Dakota, William Janklow, who was later elected governor of the state, assumed that the extradition law would be upheld and the militant leader would be returned to face a prison sentence on assault and riot convictions. California Governor Edmund G. Brown, Jr., however, denied extradition, which meant that Banks could live free in California so long as Brown was governor. Banks was a political prisoner, in a comfortable sense, because he could not leave California without fear of arrest and extradition from a state where the governor would not be so sympathetic.

Constance Matthiessen and Ron Sokol reported in the *Los Angeles Times* that Alice Lytle, the extradition secretary at the time extradition was denied, explained that the decision was based on the poor race relations in South Dakota at the time, and when you "balance that against the relatively light conviction—he wasn't convicted of murder or armed robbery, he was convicted of riot and assault without intent to kill, and these are typical charges that arise out of demonstrations—when you balance the circumstances against the need that South Dakota had to imprison him behind these charges, the danger to his life seems significant enough to refuse the extradition request."

Dennis Banks lost his pacific sanctuary when George Deukmejian was elected governor of California; he would allow extradition to South Dakota. Matthiessen and Sokol point out that, "besides the danger that Banks faces in South Dakota, Deukmejian should consider the fact that Banks has been a productive and law-abiding citizen during his time in California. . . . He has lectured at high schools and colleges throughout the state. A number of California cities have commended him for his work, and various groups have urged Deukmejian to allow Banks to stay." Banks did not take the chance; he moved from California to the Onondaga Nation, a reservation near Syracuse, New York, which claims to be a sovereign nation where neither state nor federal agents have jursidiction.

Some tribal people will continue to believe in sudden slogans and symbolic forms of protest; and there are people who are convinced that the expressions of internal rage by tribal militants were a real revolution. There are also tribal people who will continue to revise the vain advertisements of peripatetic mouth warriors as statements of traditional visions. When the word wars of the putative warriors mumble down to the last exclamation points in newspaper columns, however, the radical dramas will best be remembered in personal metaphors: the lovers at the rim of time, children late to breakfast, people touched in mythic dreams, humor in the dark parks, undone poems.

THE SHAMAN AND TERMINAL CREEDS

∎

All societies, however stable, face recurrent crises and tensions. The shaman is a kind of social safety valve who dramatizes the dise-quilibrium and employs tech-niques to reduce it, not the least of which is the dramatization itself. Like all imaginative acts, the shamanistic seance and ritual make the unknown visible and palpable, transforming anxiety into something manageable by giving it form — a name, a shape, and a way of acting as a conse-quence of this embodiment.

Eleanor Wilner,
Gathering the Winds

∎

"American Indians lack a word to denote what we call religion," writes Åke Hultkrantz in *The Religions of the American Indians*. "Of course, nothing else is to be expected in environments where religious attitudes and values permeate cultural life in its entirety and are not isolated from other cultural manifestations."

Tribal cultures did, however, denote in their languages the separa-tion between what is traditional or sacred and what is secular or profane. Tribal cultures reveal supernatural events and remember the past in oral traditional stories. The tellers of these stories were the verbal artists of the time, those who imagined in their visual memories sacred and secular events. The stories that have been recorded, translated, and printed as scripture, however, have altered tribal religious experiences. Published stories have become the standardized versions, the secular work of methodological academics; the artistic imagination has been polarized in print, and the relationships between the tellers of stories and the listeners, the visual references to the natural world, are lost in translation. The formal descriptions of tribal events by outsiders, such as missionaries, explorers, and anthropologists, reveal more about the cultural values of the observer than the imaginative power of spiritual tribal people.

SHAMANS AND THE CLERKS

■

Paul Beaulieu, who served the government as an interpreter and who was one of the first settlers at the White Earth Reservation, told about his "experiences with a *jessakkid*," a shaman or healer, in 1858 at Leech Lake. Beaulieu, a Catholic mixedblood, had little faith in the power of tribal shamans. Reports of the "wonderful performances" of the shaman, writes Walter James Hoffman in his report, "The Mide wiwin; or 'Grand Medicine Society' of the Ojibwa," published by the United States Bureau of American Ethnology, "had reached the agency, and as Beaulieu had no faith in jugglers, he offered to wager $100, a large sum, then and there, against goods of equal value, that the juggler could not perform satisfactorily one of the tricks of his repertoire. . . ." The shaman erected a lodge for the occasion. "The framework of vertical poles, inclined to the center, was filled in with interlaced twigs covered with blankets and birchbark from the ground to the top, leaving an upper orifice of about a foot in diameter for the ingress and egress of spirits and the objects to be mentioned, but not large enough for the passage of a man's body. At one side of the lower wrapping a flap was left for the entrance of the *jessakkid*.

"A committee of twelve was selected to see that no communication was possible between the *jessakkid* and confederates. These were reliable people, one of them the Episcopal clergyman of the reservation. The spectators were several hundred in number, but they stood off, not being allowed to approach.

"The *jessakkid* then removed his clothing, until nothing remained but the breechcloth. Beaulieu took a rope," which he selected for the purpose, Hoffman writes, "and first tied and knotted one end about the juggler's ankles; his knees were then securely tied together, next the wrists, after which the arms were passed over the knees and a billet of wood passed through under the knees, thus securing and keeping the arms down motionless. The rope was then passed around his neck, again and again, each time tied and knotted, so as to bring the face down upon the knees." A flat black stone from a river, the sacred spirit stone of the shaman, "was left lying upon his thighs.

"The *jessakkid* was then carried to the lodge and placed inside upon a mat on the ground, and the flap covering was restored so as to completely hide him from view.

"Immediately loud, thumping noises were heard, and the framework began to sway from side to side with great violence; whereupon the clergyman remarked that this was the work of the Evil One and 'it was no place for him,' so he left and did not see the end. After a few minutes of violent movements and swayings of the lodge accompanied by loud inarticulate noises, the motions gradually ceased when the voice of the juggler was heard, telling Beaulieu to go to the house of a friend, near by, and get the rope.

"Now, Beaulieu, suspecting some joke was to be played upon him, directed the committee to be very careful not to permit any one to approach while he went for the rope, which he found at the place indicated, still tied exactly as he had placed it about the neck and extremities of the *jessakkid*. He immediately returned, laid it down before the spectators, and requested of the *jessakkid* to be allowed to look at him, which was granted, but with the understanding that Beaulieu was not to touch him.

"When the covering was pulled aside, the *jessakkid* sat within the lodge, contentedly smoking his pipe, with no other object in sight than the black stone *manidoo*," or manitou, a spiritual stone. Beaulieu paid his wager of one hundred dollars.

"An exhibition of similar presented powers, also for a wager, was announced a short time after, at Yellow Medicine, Minnesota, to be given in the presence of a number of Army people, but at the threat of the Grand Medicine Man of the Leech Lake bands, who probably objected to interference with his lucrative monopoly, the event did not take place and bets were declared off."

Shamanism and tribal spiritual events were often explained in economic terms, the dominant metaphors of the dominant culture. Others have interpreted tribal religious events from secure carrels in libraries. Christopher Vecsey, for example, writes in his dissertation, "Traditional Ojibwa Religion and its Historical Changes," that the "Ojibwas have lost their trust in their aboriginal" *manidoog*, or manitou, the spirits, "and in themselves. . . . They have changed many of their religious rituals and today hold very few shaking tent ceremonies . . . their traditional religion no longer exists. . . . They stand between their collapsed traditional religion and Christianity, embracing neither." Vecsey seems to perceive tribal religions as museum artifacts.

William Warren, the mixedblood tribal historian, is more serious in his observations of religious events. In *History of the Ojibway Nation*, he writes that certain rites have been a secret to the whites. Some tribal healers believe that death would come to those who revealed sacred rituals. "Missionaries, travellers, and transient sojourners amongst the Ojibways, who have witnessed the performance of the grand Me-da-we

Anishinaabeg women
holding a birchbark scroll,
White Earth Reservation,
about 1939. Photo courtesy
of Minnesota Historical
Society.

ceremonies," he writes with reference to the Midewiwin, "have
represented and published that it is composed of foolish and unmeaning
ceremonies. The writer begs leave to say that these superficial observers
labor under a great mistake. The Indian has equal right . . . to say, on
viewing the rites of the Catholic and other churches, that they consist
of unmeaning and nonsensical ceremonies. There is much yet to be
learned from the wild and apparently simple son of the forest, and the
most which remains to be learned is to be derived from their religious
beliefs."

Fear of shamanic power and the unknown on the part of white people, and the fear of sorcerers and protection of the sacred on the part of
tribal healers, has increased the spiritual separation between white
observers and tribal cultures. The distance between these world views

is vast; those who venture an explanation rather than a mere description of the spiritual separation seem to reach a critical corner in narrative deductions where tribal cultures come to an end in words. Harold Hickerson, for example, writes that "Chippewa culture is a shambles, so much have the people everywhere had to accommodate to the new conditions imposed by their relations" with the white world. Nowhere, he asserts in *The Chippewa and Their Neighbors: A Study in Ethnohistory*, does the tribe depend upon goods of their own fashioning; much of the traditional material culture has been lost or "replaced and enriched by the introduction of mass-produced commodities from outside."

THE BURIAL OF JOHN KA KA GEESICK

■

The distance between tribal cultures and the white world is experienced in more than social science methodologies. One instance of cultural strain and unresolved fear of tribal spiritual rites was witnessed at the funeral of John Ka Ka Geesick, a shaman who died at the age of 124 in Warroad, Minnesota. The shaman and healer was born in 1844 and lived most of his life as a trapper and woodsman on a small land allotment on Muskeg Bay at Lake of the Woods.

The white citizens knew the old shaman from the streets; he walked into town for his supplies, for which he paid cash. John Ka Ka Geesick was known to tourists because he had posed for a photograph from which postcards were printed and sold. He was invented and colonized in the photograph, pictured in a blanket and a turkey feather headdress. On the streets of the town he wore common clothes. The feathered visage encouraged the romantic expectations of tourists. He was a town treasure, in a sense, an image from the tribal past, but when he died the mortician dressed him in a blue suit, with a white shirt and necktie. He was not buried in buckskin; he was decorated in a padded coffin, while the citizens of the town planned a ceremonial public funeral in the Warroad School Gymnasium.

Ka Ka Geesick was a man of visions and dreams; his music and world view connected him to a tribal place on the earth. He was secure at the center of his imagination and memories; in a sense, he was in a spiritual balance, blessed to live so long. The world around him, however, invented his culture and advertised his images on picture postcards. The mock headdress, and the standard burial practices, were new forms of colonization. The eldest of the tribe was possessed in photographs and public services to his grave.

Ka Ka Geesick, his legal name, is derived from *gaagige giizhig*, which means *forever* and *day*, or everlasting day, a phonetic transcription from the oral tradition of the Anishinaabeg.

Tribal people were not invited to plan the public celebration in the town. Several tribal families, however, summoned a shaman for traditional burial ceremonies. The white mortician was nervous; he was not accustomed to so much touching of the body. Later, when the coffin was closed, the mortician seemed relieved; he seemed to sigh when the coffin was lowered into the cold grave.

Daniel Raincloud, a healer and shaman from Ponemah on the Red Lake Reservation, conducted the tribal burial ceremonies. White people were invited, but none attended the traditional tribal observance. The white citizens of the town waited at a distance, separated from the tribal event by the double doors of the gymnasium. Outside, white people peered through the cracks in the doors.

"What does he have in that bundle?" a white man asked as he stepped back from the door. The shaman carried a medicine bundle.

"I really never thought there were any medicine men left," said a white woman to the others near the crack in the door.

Inside, Raincloud shook a small rattle; the sound seemed to settle the angular and uncomfortable space at the end of the gymnasium. The tribal men around the coffin sang an honoring song, and then the shaman spoke in a sacred language to *gaagige giizhig*, a path in words and music to the spirit world. Then he placed a pair of red cotton gloves and some tobacco in the coffin while the traditional elders in the circle opened a bundle that contained small finger sandwiches for the burial feast. Packages of cigarettes were opened. Raincloud pointed in the six directions, and then he passed the sandwiches to those present. The coffin was closed and turned several times on the pedestal to free the spirit of *gaagige giizhig*. They smoked cigarettes, shared the tobacco in a sacred time and place with the old shaman before he moved to the spirit world.

When the tribal burial ceremonies ended, the doors of the gymnasium were opened and the space which had been settled with the sound of a rattle was now trembling with the sound of an organ. Christian hymns replaced tribal music, and a white evangelist delivered a passionate eulogy about a man he had never seen inside his church.

John Ka Ka Geesick was buried next to his brother Na May Puk in the Highland Park Cemetery. Several tribal elders stood around the grave in the fresh snow, their feet close to the coal fires that had thawed the earth. The gravediggers waited at a distance, eager to fill the hole before the fresh soil froze.

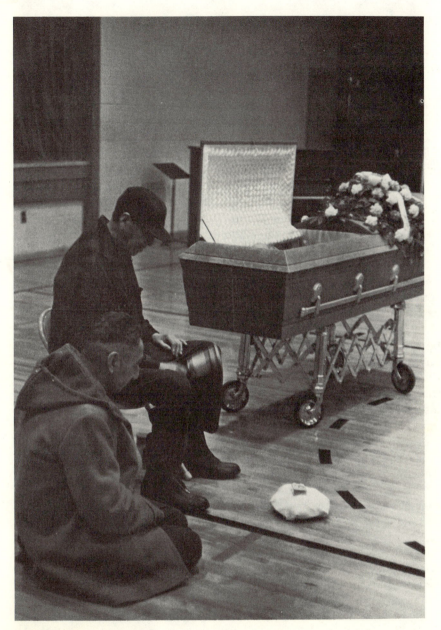

Daniel Raincloud, with
rattle, near the coffin which
bears the body of John Ka
Ka Geesick, Warroad,
Minnesota, 1968. Photo by
the author.

CORA KATHERINE SHEPPO

■

Shamanism is an uncommon religious experience that is not limited in time, place, or culture. The shaman is a person who dissolves time, establishes an ecstatic relationship with the spirit world, and learns to speak the languages of animals, birds, and plants. The shaman is a soul or spirit doctor who heals through ecstasies and contact with spirits and unusual forces in the world; the cause of most diseases is understood to be an imbalance in the individual and the world. Shamans, and other healers who have been identified as "medicine men" in the white world, seek to balance the forces in the world through ecstatic experiences: music, herbs, dreams and visions, and ceremonial dances.

There are two souls in the traditional woodland tribal world view: one is a "free soul" that travels in shadows and dreams, and the second soul is centered in the heart, the place of consciousness and emotional experiences. The "free soul" can be separated and lost.

Åke Hultkrantz points out that the "notion that a human being may be struck by enchantment or sorcery is quite common," in tribal cultures, and as "a rule the agent of diseases is a supernatural factor, and among the most widespread causes given for disease we may note enchantment, transgression of a taboo, intrusion of foreign objects or beings, and soul loss." The shaman who has experienced symbolic death, and who can dissolve familiar time and visit the dead, has the spiritual power to heal a person who suffers from soul loss. The tribal diagnosis of soul loss, Hultkrantz explains, "presupposes that the sick man's soul, generally the free soul, of its own free will or by force has left the body. At times it may have wandered off into the natural surroundings; at other times it may have been carried away by malevolent spirits, especially the dead. In such cases it is up to the shaman to send his own soul or less often, one of his guardian spirits, to retrieve the runaway soul. . . . Shamanic tales from various places describe how the shamans battle for life and death with the inhabitants of the other world, and how they are pursued by the dead on the return journey. . . ."

Cora Katherine Sheppo told the court psychiatrist that she smothered her grandchild because he had been "spawned by the devil." She said she heard a voice speak to her grandchild when she pushed a pillow down over his face. Bubas would not die, she explained with tears and fear in her eyes; he seemed to be given strength from evil forces. "It was like he could breathe right through the pillows."

Cora Sheppo wrapped her grandchild in a Pendleton blanket with an "Indian" design and delivered him dead to the Minneapolis Children's

Hospital a few blocks from her apartment. When the medical doctor uncovered the child he found two ceremonial willow sticks in his chest.

Bubas, his affectionate nickname, was baptized Tenetkoce Yahola. The child, on the afternoon of his death, was dressed in blue cotton overalls which were pulled down to the diaper at his waist. His left foot was bare, the hightop white shoe turned to the wrong side. A small bustle, with two eagle feathers, a ceremonial wooden tomahawk, a white plastic crucifix, and other religious icons were beside him on the colorful wool blanket. Tenetkoce, a tribal name, was born March 21, 1979, in Clairmore, Oklahoma. Twenty months later he was dead; and on November 4, 1980, his grandmother was arrested and charged with murder. Two months later, following a court-ordered psychiatric evaluation, Cora Sheppo waived her right to a jury trial and was found not guilty by reason of mental illness; she was committed to a state mental hospital.

Carl Malmquist, a psychiatric consultant to the district court, interviewed Cora Sheppo for several hours while she was detained in jail, and concluded in his diagnosis that the defendant suffered from a "schizophrenic disorder, paranoid type," which, according to definitions in a psychiatric lexicon, means that a person has "disturbances of thought, mood, and behavior . . . alterations of concept formation that may lead to misinterpretation of reality . . . " with the "presence of grandiose *delusions*, often associated with *hallucinations*." Cora, a mixedblood, who was forty-two years old at the time of her arrest for murder, had lived at Lac du Flambeau, Wisconsin, as a child, and later in Chicago. She has relatives who live in Kansas and Oklahoma. Cora has three children: two sons, Michael and Lauren, and a daughter, Patricia, who is the mother of Tenetkoce Yahola.

Malmquist reported to the court that Cora Sheppo "has bizarre delusions and thoughts of being controlled by external forces of the devil, and evil powers outside her. There is a feeling of her being split in terms of an external force being in control of her actions, and on that basis, her feeling is that this other-worldly force is responsible for what she felt compelled to do . . . she was required to rescue her grandson from a greater evil by killing him."

Malmquist made it clear in his evaluation that he had "no qualifications or background pertaining to Indian religious practices. I am not acquainted with any contemporary religious ceremonies which require infant sacrifice. . . ."

Julian Silverman has studied acute schizophrenic behavior and shamanic inspiration. He found no significant differences between acute schizophrenics and shamans that "define their abnormal experiences." The differences are found in the "degree of cultural acceptance of a unique resolution of a basic life crisis." In his article, "Shamans and Acute Schizophrenia," Silverman concludes that the "essential difference between the psychosocial environments of the schizophrenic and the shaman lies in the pervasiveness of the anxiety that complicates each of their lives. The emotional supports and the modes of collective solutions of the basic problems of existence available to the shaman," he writes, "greatly alleviate the strain of an otherwise excruciatingly painful existence. Such supports are all too often completely unavailable to the schizophrenic in our culture."

Cora told her daughter and the psychiatrist about the time she was drunk and drove her car off the road at high speed, a suicide attempt. Malmquist reported to the court that "it was after her attempted suicide when she also began to feel that perhaps at one time she had already died. She had an experience of feeling that she was in a tunnel and that someone had put their hands on her shoulders. She stopped and opened her eyes and in front of her was her boyfriend who had died." Loren Valliere, the man she loved, was killed in an auto accident three years earlier. "She recalled hearing him tell her to be good but at the same time, she experienced this as 'death warnings.' She felt it was an invite to rejoin him through death." Valliere and her grandson were born on the same day and month, which she thought was a spiritual connection.

Cora Sheppo was not a shaman, she was not a healer, but her experiences several months before she smothered her grandson have been diagnosed as schizophrenia and seem to be similar to those experiences associated with traditional tribal shamans. She confronted evil forces, she heard voices out of familiar time, and she told the psychiatrist that she had experienced a feeling of death, but her pain and anxieties were not supported in the dominant culture as sacred travel. Perhaps her needs for tribal connections and a sense of spiritual rebirth were manipulated by false healers and certain tribal people with political ambitions, but with incomplete, and sometimes dangerous, visions. The shaman dissolves time and expresses the inspirations of death and rebirth with cultural acceptance; and as a healer the shaman is capable of ecstatic travel in search of lost souls. Cora Sheppo needed a shaman to rescue her soul and save her grandchild.

Michael Harner, in *The Ways of the Shaman*, writes that shamanism "is a great mental and emotional adventure, one in which the patient as well as the shaman-healer are involved. Through his heroic journey and efforts, the shaman helps his patients transcend their normal, ordinary definition of reality, including the definition of themselves as ill. The shaman shows his patients that they are not emotionally and spiritually alone in their struggles against illness and death. The shaman shares his

special powers and convinces his patients, on a deep level
sciousness, that another human is willing to offer up his own self to
them. The shaman's self-sacrifice calls forth a commensurate emotiona
commitment from his patients, a sense of obligation to struggle alongside
the shaman to save one's self. Caring and curing go hand in hand."

Patricia Sheppo told William Rouleau, an investigator for the local
county attorney, that her mother had participated in peyote ceremonies
but that she had not become serious about tribal spiritual events until
she took part in The Longest Walk, a protest march across the nation to
focus attention on tribal issues. She participated in purification ceremonies
in a sweat lodge and she forbore the use of alcohol and drugs. Cora told
the psychiatrist that she had been baptized and confirmed a Roman
Catholic, but, the psychiatrist reported to the court, "she now liked to
think of her religion as being that of a 'traditional Indian religion.' I asked
her what that involved, and she stated they are always obedient to the
Creator, and people have it written into them in terms of how they are
supposed to be. 'We know there's one thing above all and that's not to
criticize. I fall far short from my tendencies to do bad things like go to
taverns and play pool, but I don't drink, lie or gossip. I would never do
anything to dishonor my Lord and Savior. Morning Star is the son of
God. He is Jesus, the light and shining star. The reservation which I left
had very little of the traditional Indian things left. Nothing has been
passed on. All that's left is drinking and I used to do it, too. All else is
forgotten when they drink.'

"It was at that point that I asked," Malmquist reported to the court,
". . . whether she could tell me more about what some of these experiences might have been and if they were connected with the death
of Bubas. She replied, 'He was the spawn of the devil and no one and
nothing will ever change my mind.' She looked directly at me in stating
this, had a look of fixed determination in her eyes, voice and face as she
stated it. It had the tone of being put to me as though asking me to
challenge it since she would never change her mind." Cora said she realized this on the day her grandson died. "It was not that she had not been
having various thoughts about the devil and evil mixed in with the
'powers' before that, but rather that until that day, she had felt that Bubas
could be protected by prayer. On that morning she took him out 'into
a field' which was apparently a playground near their house. While at
the playground, she prayed with him, asking the Creator for strength
and to save him from the evil one. She would not tell me what the specific
signs were over time that had made her suspect that Bubas had been
'spawned by the devil,' but she told me she had handled her suspicions
by 'putting them out of my mind by prayer.' She repeated her conviction

ned by the devil several times. 'I knew it. I didn't
. No one can convince me otherwise.'

th Bubas in the playground," Malmquist continued
court, "it dawned on her what she had to do. She
going back to her home and taking Bubas upstairs.

'I u ..... grandson dead than possessed by the devil. Before
that day, I suspected he was spawned by the devil but I put it aside. That
day it came out of nowhere. I knew it. I couldn't doubt it. My only regret
was that he was my grandson. I would have had to do it to anyone when
directed. I don't go around killing little kids.'

"When I asked her why it happened at that particular time, she was
not able to tell me, but could only emphasize, as she did many times,
that it was overpowering to her and she had not felt able to resist the
forces that were making her do it . . . the act was actually under the control of these powers, but it was also done for Bubas. 'All I know is that
I was bound and determined to fight for him. He was my grandson and
I was doing this for him. When I got into my apartment, I realized right
away what I had to do. I couldn't stop until it was done. I wanted to make
him sleep as painless as possible. He was going to grow up to be the
ultimate power of evil. Only the Creator would have been able to stop
him.' She then elaborated her belief that the Creator had picked her to
do this job. . . ."

Nelson Sheppo, father of Cora, who lived at Lac du Flambeau,
Wisconsin, when he was interviewed, revealed that his daughter had also
attended Sun Dance ceremonies. He said that the "Indian religion is
something else that a lot of them don't understand, and she don't understand . . . see the Indian religion is strictly believing in the Almighty God.
The Holy Spirit they call it. Manitou they call it," or *manidoo*.

"Do you know what that means?"

"Manitou, that's who it is, the Great Spirit. That's God Almighty.
See, the Indian never knew Jesus Christ when He was born. They often
wondered why that star, bright star. . . . They didn't know what it meant,
until the white man come, see. That's what I tell about, like I go on nar-
rating in schools all over the country and I talk about that, see. The Indian didn't know who Jesus Christ was until the white man come."

"You said that she didn't understand the Indian religion?"

"Well . . . to tell the truth she don't understand the drum religion.
See, that's the Indian religion, and that's strict. . . . The Indian chief
always got up and they said we always ask the Great Spirit to bless us,
keep us, that we should be thankful that he gave us everything on this
earth that we eat, wild game, wild potatoes, wild turnips, wild celery,
all that, everything that's on this earth, that's who gave it to us, the Great

Spirit. . . . A lot of professors always say that the Indian went on this hill to talk to the trees maybe, to talk to the rocks, but that's untrue. He goes up there and asks the Great Spirit for blessings. Then, when they used to do that, see."

"Cora didn't understand that . . . ?"

"No, she never . . . I tried to tell her."

Patricia Sheppo told the investigator that she dreamed about the death of her child two weeks before he died. She said she dreamed that he was playing on a slide in a park when "he just died, ya know, and there was nothing I could do about it. . . . I thought the warning was for me to straighten up, ya know, and start spending a lot more time with him . . . and so I started straightening up and then two weeks after that. . . ."

Patricia said that she met the father of her child on The Longest Walk, and that she too became more active in tribal spiritual events. When the investigator asked her if she or her mother had ever come in contact with "bad medicine," she replied that she was not sure. Later, however, she described several unusual events that troubled her enough to remember them. At the Black Hills Alliance, a survival gathering which was held four years ago in South Dakota, Patricia told the investigator about a meeting where the women formed a circle and joined hands. "And then, I don't know, there was a few chants that they were singing, *we are witches, we are women, and there is no beginning, there is no end* . . . that's the way their songs started. And then they were humming, like hummmmm for a real long time, ya know. . . ."

"Is that typical among Indian ladies?"

"No. . . . It was really different, ya know, and I was really, ya know, I thought, what are they doing, ya know, cause I had never . . . I felt really bad because I felt like I had failed trying to get to them about having some self-respect, and right after I got done telling them that, a lot of women started taking off their shirts and walking around braless and stuff, so I just thought wow, ya know, it just kinda blew my mind. . . ."

"What did your mother say about those women?"

"She told me they were witches," she responded.

Earlier in the summer, Patricia said, "a lot of strange things" happened around her apartment where she lived with her son, her mother, and two younger brothers. "Ya know, this really weird black cat started hanging around the house . . . and I didn't like that at all." Once, while she was on a bus, she found a sheet of paper with her name on it, and "it just totally freaked me out because of all the strange things" that had happened. Cora told her to burn the paper.

"What did your mother think it was?"

"My mom thought it was some people trying to get at me, ya know,"

she told the investigator. "Like the cult or something trying to get me. . . .
I am a really strong person, ya know, as far as willpower is concerned. . . .
I really couldn't understand why they would be wanting to get at me,
ya know."

Patricia and the father of her child were concerned about the adverse
influences of a cult; a friend and tribal counselor was invited to search
their apartment for possible causes of "bad medicine." The counselor said
in an interview with an official investigator for the county that he purified
himself with sage before he entered the apartment. "We were looking
for a red jacket. . . . One of the methods in bad medicine is the exchange
of some kind of clothes. . . . We had located the red jacket and in the
pocket of that jacket we also found dried fish from the smoked fish that
was placed in their freezer. . . . Cora had told Patty not to eat that fish
at all," because it was "being used against them. . . ." The counselor said
he also found a "willow wreath that was wrapped like it was some kind
of a crown." He also found a pouch filled with a substance similar to tobacco but not a known hallucinogenic plant, and a small painted stick which
was believed to be used in adverse medicine practices. "At that point we
were instructed to burn these objects by the medicine man so that these
objects would not influence any more people. . . ."

Cora told the tribal counselor a month after she had smothered her
grandchild that there was something in the apartment. Before the incident, the counselor reported, "she was feeling something in that
house. . . . She was hoping that Patty would come home immediately
to help her through this thing. She told me that she was feeling somewhat
better when she went outside. She went back into the house and I asked
her which room in the house . . . did you feel this thing happen. . . .
Where did it happen? She told me in the living room. At that point, I
told her that there was medicine that was near that living room and in
fact we had found different medicines in different rooms. . . . I believe
she told me she placed the child on the floor. . . . she said she had tried
to stab the baby in the stomach . . . but she said she hit something that
sounded like a metal plate. . . . I believe she said she tried to choke this
thing, this being with her hands, but when she got her hands around
the being's neck the being started getting larger. That its neck muscles
started bulging and she felt or saw that this thing was expanding in nature.
Pulsating, so as to speak. . . . She was leading up to the point where
she used the Sun Dance stakes. . . . [She said] I was using these sacred
objects to drive out and kill that spirit, that devil, that being. And she
said that is when it died, when I used the Sun Dance stakes. She said
these Sun Dance stakes are sacred, they are powerful. I got those from

Anishinaabe grave houses,
Leech Lake Reservation.
Photo by the author.

the Sun Dance, they're powerful. She said people, a lot of people won't understand that. . . ."

Patricia was at college that afternoon when she was told her child was in the hospital. She remembered her dream two weeks earlier about his death as she hurried to be at his side. "I just *screamed*, and I seen my mom and I asked her what happened? 'What happened to my baby?' and she said, 'Pat, I don't know.' I said, 'I want to see him, I want to see my baby,' and so I went into this room, the emergency room, and then I seen him laying there, with the sticks in him, and I didn't known what to do. God, all I'd do was hold him and tell him how much I loved him, you know, and, and I said the words *I love you so much*, and I couldn't understand why, why it happened. . . ."

EPILOGUE
.

> *Once in his life a man man ought*
> *to concentrate his mind upon the*
> *remembered earth, I believe. He*
> *ought to give himself up to a par-*
> *ticular landscape in his exper-*
> *ience, to look at it from as many*
> *angles as he can, to wonder about*
> *it, to dwell upon it.*
>   N. Scott Momaday,
> The Way to Rainy Mountain

■

Naanabozho, the compassionate tribal trickster, imagined the earth, animals, men, women, evil spirits, birds, death, and white people. These imaginative events were told in traditional tribal creation stories and several versions were recorded by an unusual mixedblood anthropologist.

Now, when the earth was under water, as the event of the flood was told and translated, Naanabozho was perched on a great raft with his younger brother. "We will create the earth," Naanabozho said in good humor. When the earth was finished the trickster and his brother created some people for the earth so they would not have to live alone with their own trickeries. A man was imagined first, and then animals and every kind of creature. Then Naanabozho created *maji manidoog*, or evil spirits, and when he finished with that he told man to find a clear place on the earth to live. The trickster then created a woman, and then birds, and then he created white people so that he and his brother, and men and women, would not have to live alone. "No matter who or how poor one of them may be," said the first tribal creator and trickster about white people, "they shall purchase land one from another." This version was recorded and translated by William Jones and published by the American Ethnological Society.

Jones was born more than a century ago on the Sauk and Fox Reservation in Indian Territory. His tribal dream name was Megasiawa, which means Black Eagle in translation. His white mother died when he was one year old and he was cared for by his paternal tribal grandmother. Later, in a letter, Jones wrote that his "grandmother had the gift of healing . . . she knew the medicinal values of many roots and herbs, and could brew from them remedies for various disorders external and internal."

Henry Milner Rideout published a romantic tribute to his friend from Harvard University. In *William Jones: Indian, Cowboy, American Scholar, and Anthropologist in the Field*, he wrote that "his eyes—brown as his hair, with speckles of golden light in them—had a habit of looking off into distance; at which times they turned impenetrably sad, became almost the eyes of an Indian, and gave to his other features the look of stillness, far-off preoccupation, and sober dignity that is seen in the higher type of Indian countenance."

Jones attended Hampton Institute, Phillips Andover, and graduated from Harvard University. He earned his Doctor of Philosophy degree in anthropology from Columbia University. Jones was killed by tribal people while on a field trip in the Philippine Islands.

Jones recorded hundreds of Anishinaabeg stories, which were told in tribal communities and recorded at Fort William, Ontario, and at Bois Fort and Leech Lake in Minnesota, Turtle Mountain, North Dakota, and on other reservations. These stories are about mythic events, adventures, secular reversals, and animal transformations of the trickster and his relatives. How ironic it seems now that this sensitive mixedblood anthropologist, who studied with the celebrated scholar Franz Boas, was murdered by tribal people.

The Governor-General in the Philippine Islands, wrote that "it seems like the irony of fate that he should have been made away with by Ilongots after he had done so much to help and protect them. . . . When I first heard of his death and learned that it was ascribed to Ilongots . . . with whom I knew that he had lived on friendly terms, the idea immediately occurred to me that the real murderers might not improbably be the Christian natives, whose abuse of the wild people he had reported."

The transcriptions, translations, notes, and interpretations of the Anishinaabeg stories that he had recorded over a three-year period in tribal communities were with him when he died. The Field Museum of Natural History in Chicago, which sponsored his research in the Philippine Islands, rescued his manuscripts. One of the most important collections of recorded woodland stories, translated by a mixedblood scholar, was published with funds provided by the Carnegie Institute.

Jones had not completed the manuscript, not even the preface to his two-volume work, but in notes he wrote that his "work is to be taken largely as an attempt to get at the religious ideas of the people from their own point of view. . . . The language of most of the material is conversational . . . sentences colloquial, seldom sustained, and often loose and incoherent. Vagueness of reference is common. . . ."

Fort William, Ontario, July 22, 1903: Jones writes that he "went straight for the Indian reservation, which is about two miles from here. I found the people exceedingly mild and kind, which was only in keeping with what I have found among these Ojibways all along. I never saw Indians so willing, so kind in their hospitality. I met an old French half-blood, Penassie by name, who took me round among the people. He will make some things for me, traps to catch bear, skunk, mink, and so on, and other things in the way of games and the like. . . ."

Jones reveals that Penassie, who he thought was a genius, an artist at telling stories, "took me out to walk with him and showed me some of his realm. In a moment of extreme friendliness he let fall some remarks to the effect that he wished I would come and live here, take to myself a wife and be one of the people. . . ." Jones never married.

Joe Morrison served as his interpreter while he was at Leech Lake in Minnesota. Jones visited tribal people from Bear Island who had invited him out to witness a medicine dance of the Midewiwin. "A vast amount of excellent myth material," he wrote. He also recorded trickster stories told by Ten Claws near Lake Vermillion at Bois Fort in Minnesota. "It is good stuff, and I am proud of it."

In one of his last letters from the Philippine Islands, Jones wrote to a colleague that he would present the tales of the Anishinaabeg "as they come from the lips of the narrator, and my manuscript will be arranged that both text and translation can be published at the same time . . . of course you know this is rather for science than for popular reading, and it was better so; for much of it is naive and unrestrained, and it wades with childish simplicity through what so-called civilized people term indelicacy."

Jones translated the following narrative, which was told in the oral tradition more than eighty years ago. This short narrative, with hundreds of other stories recorded in Ontario, Canada, and in Minnesota, was collected and published by the American Ethnological Society.

THE SPIRIT WORLD
■

Something else I will relate concerning what the people of old have said. Whenever any one died, it was common for him to rise from the dead; and so he would give an account of what it was like at the place where the dead go. A very large road leads to the place where go those who have died. A great many one saw walking straight west where leads the road.

First one found some large blueberries hanging aloft, some raspberries too. If any one ate them, not again would one return home. At last one saw where the great river was, very swift was its current. And then there one saw a log lying across the stream, unfastened lay the log. Very dangerous it was; some fell off from the log there. And the one that succeeded in crossing the log was able to go over to the ghostly region. Next one saw dogs there that were eager to bite one. And all sorts of things they all saw after they had crawled across. Next an old woman one saw, a stick in her hand the old woman held. Concerning all sorts of things one was questioned, some how one had lived. Some of them the old woman did not let pass; some of them she hit; and some without annoyance she let go on to the spirit-world. And after one had arrived there where the ghosts were, they were found living in a great town. When one arrived at the place, one saw many who had been related to one in the past. A very big dance they had together in the silence of the night. They whistled, they whooped. If any one had on this earth became mindful of one whom one was related to in the past, and if one placed food in a vessel or put it on the fire, then over there would arrive the food which one fed to one that had been a relative.

In various forms appeared they who danced, even upon their heads they stood when they danced. And this was why the people of old used to say whenever anybody died: "Don't ask anybody to accompany you." They pointed out to one the way straight towards the west. "Now, straight in that direction do you go," they said to one. "There in that place you will come to where the ghosts have a town." All kinds of things they gave to one; in the same manner as when one was fitted out for a journey, so they fitted one out. A knife, tobacco, pipe, fire, and a little food, they placed there for the dead.

And then there at the grave they sometimes kindled a fire and cooked food, when they were mindful of one that had died. Food, tobacco, and fire they placed there. And then over there at the place where the ghosts were arrived the food.

There was one great ghostly person who watched over the ghosts, for such was what I have heard people of old say. Sometimes the great ghostly man sent one back to the earth. "Not yet is your time us to come to this place." And this was the occasion when one sometimes came back to life.

BIBLIOGRAPHY

■

BOOKS ABOUT THE ANISHINAABEG

BIBLIOGRAPHY: BOOKS ABOUT THE ANISHINAABEG

■

There are hundreds of books, and several hundred articles and reports, published about the Anishinaabeg, or the Chippewa and Ojibway, and other related woodland tribal families. The most useful list of written materials on the Anishinaabeg was prepared by Helen Hornbeck Tanner for the Newberry Library. The list of books here includes recommended titles, other books about tribal cultures, and titles mentioned in the text of this book.

RECOMMENDED TITLES
■

Baraga, Friedric.
   1966   *A Dictionary of the Otchipwe Language.* Minneapolis: Ross and Haines. First published in 1878 and 1880 in Cincinnati and Montreal.

Barnouw, Victor.
   1977   *Wisconsin Chippewa Myths & Tales.* Madison: The University of Wisconsin Press.

Brill, Charles.
   1974   *Indian and Free; A Contemporary Portrait of Life on a Chippewa Reservation.* Minneapolis: University of Minnesota Press.

Coleman, Sister Bernard; Frogner, Ellen; and Eich, Estelle.
   1962   *Ojibwa Myths and Legends.* Minneapolis: Ross and Haines.

Copway, George; Kahgegagahbowh.
   1847   *The Life, History, and Travels of Kah-ge-ga-gah-bowh.* Philadelphia: James Harmstead.

Copway, George; Kahgegagahbowh.
   1850   *The Traditional History and Characteristic Sketches of the Ojibway Nation.* London: Charles Gilpin.

Densmore, Frances.
   1971   *Chippewa Customs.* Minneapolis: Ross and Haines. First published by the

Smithsonian Institution, Bureau of American Ethnology, Bulletin 86, United
States Government Printing Office.

Densmore, Frances.
1974 *Chippewa Music*. Minneapolis: Ross and Haines. First published, in two
volumes, by the Smithsonian Institution, Bureau of American Ethnology,
Bulletins 45 and 53, United States Government Printing Office.

Dewdney, Selwyn.
1975 *The Sacred Scrolls of the Southern Ojibway*. Toronto: University of Toronto
Press. Published for the Glenbow-Alberta Institute, Calgary, Alberta.

Dewdney, Selwyn; and Kidd, Kenneth E.
1962 *Indian Rock Paintings of the Great Lakes*. Toronto: University of Toronto Press.
Published for the Quetico Foundation.

Hoffman, Walter James.
1891 "The Mide wiwin; or 'Grand Medicine Society' of the Ojibwa," in *United
States Bureau of American Ethnology. Seventh Annual Report, 1885-86*. Government Printing Office.

Jones, Peter; Kahkewaquonaby.
1861 *History of the Ojebway Indians; With Especial Reference to Their Conversion to
Christianity*. London: A. W. Bennet.

Jones, William.
1917 *Ojibwa Texts*. Collected by William Jones and edited by Truman Michelson.
Leyden: E. J. Brill. Publications of the American Ethnological Society.

Landes, Ruth.
1968 *Ojibway Religion and the Midéwiwin*. Madison: The University of Wisconsin Press.

McKenney, Thomas Loraine.
1827 *Sketches of a Tour of the Lakes, of the Character and Customs of the Chippeway
Indians, and of Incidents Connected With the Treaty of Fond du Lac*. Baltimore:
Fielding Lucas. Reprinted by Imprint Society, 1972.

Nichols, John; and Nyholm, Earl, editors.
1979 *Ojibwewi-Ikidowinan: An Ojibwe Word Resource Book*. Word contributors:
Maude Kegg, Earl Nyholm, and Selam Ross. Saint Paul: Minnesota Arch-
aeological Society.

Rogers, John.
1973 *Red World and White: Memories of a Chippewa Boyhood*. Norman: University
of Oklahoma Press. First published as *A Chippewa Speaks*, 1957.

Tanner, Helen Hornbeck.
1976 *The Ojibwas: A Critical Bibliography*. Bloomington: Indiana University Press.
Published for the Newberry Library.

Tanner, John.
1956 *A Narrative of the Captivity and Adventure of John Tanner*. Edited by Edwin
James. Minneapolis: Ross and Haines. First published in New York, 1830.

Vizenor, Gerald.
1981 *Earthdivers: Tribal Narratives on Mixed Descent*. Minneapolis: University of
Minnesota Press.

Vizenor, Gerald.
1978 *Wordarrows: Indians and Whites in the New Fur Trade.* Minneapolis: University of Minnesota Press.

Warren, William Whipple.
1957 *History of the Ojibway Nation.* Minneapolis: Ross and Haines. First published by the Minnesota Historical Society, 1885.

OTHER BOOKS ABOUT TRIBAL CULTURES AND TITLES
MENTIONED IN THE TEXT
■

Astrov, Margot.
1946 *The Winged Serpent.* New York: John Day.

Barnes, Nellie.
1921 *American Indian Verse.* Lawrence, Kansas: Bulletin of University of Kansas, volume 22, number 18.

Berg, Sister Carol.
1981 "Climbing Learners; Hill: Benedictines at White EArth, 1878-1945." Unpublished dissertation, University of Minnesota.

Berkhofer, Robert F., Jr.
1981 *The White Man's Indians: Images of the American Indian from Columbus to the Present.* New York: Alfred A. Knopf.

Billington, Ray Allen.
1981 *Land of Savagery Land of Promise: The European Image of the American Frontier in the Nineteenth Century.* New York: W. W. Norton & Company.

Brown, Jennifer S. H.
1980 *Strangers in Blood: Fur Trade Company Families in Indian Country.* Vancouver: University of British Columbia Press.

Danziger, Edmund Jefferson.
1978 *The Chippewa of Lake Superior.* Norman: University of Oklahoma Press.

Denevan, William, editor.
1976 *The Native Population of the Americas in 1492.* Madison: The University of Wisconsin Press.

Dobyns, Henry F.
1976 *Native American Historical Demography: A Critical Bibliography.* Bloomington; Indiana University Press. Published for the Newberry Library.

Douglas, Mary.
1973 *Natural Symbols: Explorations in Cosmology.* London: Barrie and Jenkins.

Drinnon, Richard.
1980 *Facing West: The Metaphysics of Indian-Hating and Empire-Building.* Minneapolis: University of Minnesota Press.

Eliade, Mircea.
1982 *Ordeal by Labyrinth.* Conversations with Claude-Henri Rocquet. Chicago: The University of Chicago Press.

Everett, Michael; and Waddell, Jack, editors.
  1980 *Drinking Behavior among Southwestern Indians.* Tucson: University of Arizona Press.

Gould, Stephen Jay.
  1981 *The Mismeasure of Man.* New York: W. W. Norton & Company.

Harner, Michael.
  1980 *The Way of the Shaman.* New York: Harper & Row.

Hickerson, Harold.
  1970 *The Chippewa and Their Neighbors: A Study in Ethnohistory.* New York: Holt, Rinehart and Winston.

Hill, Thomas Warren.
  1976 " 'Feeling Good' and 'Getting High': Alcohol Use of Urban Indians." Unpublished dissertation, University of Pennsylvania.

Hultkrantz, Åke.
  1981 *Belief and Worship in Native North America.* Syracuse: Syracuse University Press.

Hultkrantz, Åke.
  1979 *The Religions of the American Indians.* Berkeley: University of California Press.

Jamison, James K.
  1946 *By Cross and Anchor: The Story of Frederic Baraga on Lake Superior.* Paterson, New Jersey: St. Anthony Guild Press.

Kroeber, Karl, editor.
  1981 *Traditional Literatures of the American Indian.* Lincoln: University of Nebraska Press.

Larsen, Stephen.
  1976 *The Shaman's Doorway: Opening the Mythic Imagination to Contemporary Consciousness.* New York: Harper & Row.

Lender, Mark Edward; and Martin, James Kirby.
  1982 *Drinking in America.* New York: The Free Press, Collier MacMillan Publishers.

Lurie, Nancy Oestreich.
  1971 "The World's Oldest On-Going Protest Demonstration: North American Indian Drinking Patterns." *Pacific Historical Review,* volume 60, number 3, August 1971.

MacAndrew, Craig; and Edgerton, Robert B.
  1969 *Drunken Comportment: A Social Explanation.* Chicago: Aldine Publishing Company.

Martin, Calvin.
  1978 *Keepers of the Game: Indian-Animal Relationships and the Fur Trade.* Berkeley: University of California Press.

Miller, Michael; and Wittstock, Laura Waterman.
  1981 "Indian Alcoholism in Saint Paul." *Center for Urban and Regional Affairs Report,* University of Minnesota, November 1981.

Morrison, Eliza.
  1978 *A Little History of My Forest Life.* La Crosse, Wisconsin: Sumac Press.

Morton, Samuel George.
   1839   *Crania Americana*. Philadelphia: John Pennington.

Ong, Walter J.
   1982   *Orality and Literacy: The Technologizing of the Word*. London: Methuen.

Paredes, J. Anthony, editor.
   1980   *Anishinabe: 6 Studies of Modern Chippewa*. Tallahassee; University Presses of Florida.

Rideout, Henry Milner.
   1912   *William Jones: Indian, Cowboy, American Scholar, and Anthropologist in the Field*. New York: Frederick A. Stokes.

Ross, Hamilton Nelson.
   1960   *La Pointe—Village Outpost*. Printed by Edward Brothers in Ann Arbor, Michigan.

Silverman, Julian.
   1967   "Shamans and Acute Schizophrenia." *American Anthropologist*.

Slotkin, Richard.
   1973   *Regeneration Through Violence*. Middletown, Connecticut: Wesleyan University Press.

Thornton, Russel; Sandefur, Gary; and Grasmick, Harold.
   1982   *The Urbanization of American Indians: A Critical Bibliography*. Bloomington: Indiana University Press. Published for the Newberry Library.

Turner, Frederick.
   1980   *Beyond Geography: The Western Spirit Against the Wilderness*. New York: The Viking Press.

Unger, Steven, editor.
   1977   *The Destruction of American Indian Families*. New York: Association of American Indian Affairs.

United States Congress.
   1887   Senate. Committee on Indian Affairs. *Testimony in Relation to Affairs at the White Earth Reservation, Minnesota*. Subcommittee hearing: Tuesday, March 8, 1887.

United States Congress.
   1976   Senate. Committee on the Judiciary. Subcommittee to Investigate the Administration of the Internal Security Act. *Revolutionary Activities Within the United States: The American Indian Movement*. Ninety-fourth Congress, Second Session. Hearing, April 6, 1976. Report, September 1976, Government Printing Office.

United States District Court.
   1974   Transcript of Trial Proceedings before Federal Judge Fred Nichol: Tuesday, February 12, 1974, Saint Paul, Minnesota. Testimony of Russell Means and Dennis Banks, pages 3909-3977.

Vaillant, George.
   1983   *The Natural History of Alcoholism*. Cambridge: Harvard University Press.

Vecsey, Christopher Thomas.
   1977   "Traditional Ojibwa Religion and its Historical Changes." Unpublished dissertation, Northwestern University.

Vecsey, Christopher; and Venables, Robert, editors.
  1980 *American Indian Environments: Ecological Issues in Native American History.*
  Syracuse: Syracuse University Press.

Vick, Judith Anola.
  1977 "The Press and Wounded Knee, 1973: An Analysis of the Coverage of the
  Occupation by Selected Newspapers and News Magazines." Unpublished thesis, University of Minnesota.

Vizenor, Gerald.
  1968 *Escorts to White Earth.* Minneapolis: Four Winds.

Vizenor, Gerald.
  1972 *The Everlasting Sky: New Voices from the People Named the Chippewa.* New
  York: Crowell-Collier Press.

Vizenor, Gerald.
  1981 *Summer in the Spring: Ojibwe Lyric Poems and Tribal Stories.* Minneapolis:
  The Nodin Press. First published in limited hardbound edition, May 1965.

Vizenor, Gerald.
  1976 *Tribal Scenes and Ceremonies.* Minneapolis: The Nodin Press.

Wagner, Roy.
  1981 *The Invention of Culture.* Chicago: The University of Chicago Press.

Westermeyer, Joseph.
  1974 " 'The Drunken Indian': Myths and Realities." *Psychiatric Annals,* volume
  4, number 11, November 1974. Reprinted in *The Destruction of American Indian Families,* edited by Steven Unger.

Wilner, Eleanor.
  1975 *Gathering the Winds: Visionary Imagination and Radical Transformation of Self
  and Society.* Baltimore: The Johns Hopkins University Press.

Zweig, Paul.
  1974 *The Adventurer.* Princeton: Princeton University Press.

INDEX

∎

INDEX

Gerald Vizenor has worked as a journalist, a community advocate for tribal people, and a teacher. He directed the first Indian studies program at Bemidji State University and served for six years on the faculty of the University of Minnesota, in the departments of American Indian Studies and American Studies. He now teaches Native American literature at the University of California, Berkeley. Vizenor is the author of *Wordarrows: Indians and Whites in the New Fur Trade* and *Earthdivers: Tribal Narratives on Mixed Descent*, both published by the University of Minnesota Press, and a prize-winning screenplay, *Harold of Orange*. His latest book is *Matsushima*, a collection of original haiku. Vizenor is a mixedblood member of the Minnesota Chippewa Tribe.